PROMETHEUS UNBOUND
AN INTERPRETATION

PROMETHEUS UNBOUND
AN INTERPRETATION

By

CARL GRABO

GORDIAN PRESS, INC.
NEW YORK
1968

Originally Published 1935

Reprinted 1968

Library of Congress Catalogue Card Number 68 19149

Published by GORDIAN PRESS with the Permission of

The University of North Carolina Press

FOREWORD

THE BACKGROUND to the *Prometheus Unbound,* its sources in philosophy and science, I wished to set before Shelley students in a generous body of appendices, including selections from neo-Platonists and others whose works are not easily accessible. But a book on such a scale is not feasible at this time. Nor is it feasible, likewise, to publish the text of the poem as edited by my friend Mr. Martin J. Freeman. Perhaps at some happier time this more comprehensive and useful book will be sufficiently in demand to justify the cost of its printing. The world's interest in Shelley's philosophy is not, at this writing, great. It is as a lyric poet only, or as a baffling personality, that Shelley is known to most readers of poetry, some among whom even resent the effort to establish him as a thinker of importance, and to interpret his longer poems in the light of philosophy.

Shelley was, nevertheless, a thinker of very great importance indeed, one whose thought was so far in advance of his time that it is only to-day that it can be understood by any great number of persons. In *Prometheus Unbound* Shelley has reconciled neo-Platonism with the advanced scientific speculation of his day and with the radical social philosophy which underlay the French Revolutionary period. He has sought to find amid the determinism of science a place for the freedom of the moral will. And he has seen the universe endlessly evolving, as God, or the One, Himself endlessly evolves.

This all has a strangely modern ring. Shelley, it would seem, is up-to-date in his philosophical speculations and has something to offer the perplexed modern world for its guidance. Were *Prometheus Unbound* merely a problem, a riddle to solve, it would have, for me, very little interest. It is because its thought is very much alive and helpful to those now

[v]

troubled by the problems which perturbed Shelley, that the decipherment of the poem repays effort. Not only is it great poetry, but philosophy also, in the high and vital sense as a guide to life.

Philosophical poems which are both good poetry and good philosophy are rare. I know of none in English comparable to *Prometheus Unbound*. Only in Lucretius and Dante, I believe, are to be found writers Shelley's equals both as poets and thinkers. But whereas the thought of Lucretius and Dante is for us outmoded, this is not true of Shelley. His problem was essentially ours and his solution is valid to-day.

These are large assertions but are soberly made, and, I trust, justified by this book. It is unlikely that my interpretation will be everyone's. A poem such as *Prometheus Unbound* is more than a philosophical disquisition. Not one but many meanings may be got from it. By this I do not say that the possible interpretations are conflicting, or that its essential thesis is capable of contradictory readings, but that the emphasis, the significance attached to this or that part of it, will vary with the individual reader. This is as it should be. But though the implications I read into the poem may not be everyone's, the interpretation of the symbols employed and the explanations of scientific and philosophic origins which I offer, are, I trust, sufficiently proved.

The proofs would be largely augmented could I incorporate in the book the copious appendices which I have prepared. The most critical points, however, are supported by citations in the text, and the larger scientific and philosophic background is partly set forth in two earlier books, *A Newton Among Poets,* and *The Meaning of the Witch of Atlas.* In the latter is much explanation of symbol, and, from the neo-Platonists, much citation bearing directly upon *Prometheus Unbound.*

I have many persons to thank for aid given in one way or another in the preparation of this book: to Cloantha Copass Kennedy, to Anna Gates Butler, to Martin J. Freeman in particular. There are, too, the many students in my graduate classes in the University of Chicago who in years past have aided in the unraveling of the poem. I trust that their pleasure in recalling our common enterprise is as great as my own. I remember still the remark of one who, when we had spent a long time wrestling with the poem's thought, exclaimed "This is a very beautiful poem!" We had said nothing of the poem's beauty, nor have I said much if anything of beauty in the ensuing pages. I like to think that an appreciation of its beauty comes best as one seeks the poem's meaning. Without understanding, the beauty perceived is superficial. With understanding and a perception of that beauty which lies deeper than felicity of phrase, can much, profitably, be said?

CARL GRABO

University of Chicago

TABLE OF CONTENTS

PROMETHEUS UNBOUND
AN INTERPRETATION

INTRODUCTION

I

SHELLEY remarks in his preface to *Prometheus Unbound* that he does not attempt to replace the lost play of Aeschylus which depicted the Titan as reconciled with Zeus. "I was," he says, "averse from a catastrophe so feeble as that of reconciling the Champion with the Oppressor of mankind. The moral interest of the fable, which is so powerfully sustained by the sufferings and endurance of Prometheus, would be annihilated if we could conceive of him as unsaying his high language and quailing before his successful and perfidious adversary." He goes on to say that "the only imaginary being resembling in any degree Prometheus, is Satan: and Prometheus is, in my judgment, a more poetical character than Satan, because, in addition to courage, and majesty, and firm and patient opposition to omnipotent force, he is susceptible of being described as exempt from the taints of ambition, envy, revenge, and a desire for personal aggrandisement, which, in the Hero of Paradise Lost, interfere with the interest. . . . But Prometheus is, as it were, the type of the highest perfection of moral and intellectual nature, impelled by the purest and the truest motives to the best and noblest ends."

That Shelley was aware of the unusual character of some of his imagery is evident: "The imagery which I have employed will be found, in many instances, to have been drawn from the operations of the human mind, or from those external actions by which they are expressed." Such imagery, he observes, though found in Shakespeare and Dante is rare in modern poetry. It was habitually employed by the Greeks "and it is the study of their works (since a higher merit would probably be denied me), to which I am willing that my readers should impute this singularity."

[3]

It is in his discussion of the poetic character of his own age and of the common body of ideas and imagery from which writers, however diverse, must draw, that Shelley twice employs a metaphor of peculiar significance in view of his imagery in the poem. "Thus a number of writers possess the form, whilst they want the spirit of those whom, it is alleged, they imitate; because the former is the endowment of the age in which they live, and the latter must be the *uncommunicated lightning* of their own mind." [Italics mine.] And again: "The great writers of our own age are, we have reason to suppose, the companions and forerunners of some unimagined change in our social condition, or the opinions which cement it. The *cloud of mind is discharging its collected lightning, and the equilibrium between institutions and opinions* is now restoring, or is about to be restored." [Italics mine.] Inasmuch as an intelligible reading of *Prometheus Unbound* turns upon an interpretation of the symbols of cloud and lightning, symbols which Shelley employs both physically of natural forces and metaphysically of the generation of souls and the passions of love and hate, his use of these in his preface indicates his preoccupation with them. Even more, perhaps, in them he hints at the hidden meaning of his parable, and offers us a key thereto.

Mrs. Shelley's note on *Prometheus Unbound*, supplied to her edition of the poems, has several valuable comments which aid in deciphering the allegory. Yet the note is more remarkable for what it does not give; for what, it is evident, Mrs. Shelley was unable to give. She says, indeed: "It requires a mind as subtle and penetrating as his own to understand the mystic meanings scattered throughout the poem. They elude the ordinary reader by their abstraction and delicacy of distinction, but they are far from vague. It was his design to write prose metaphysical essays on the nature of Man, which would have served to explain much of what is obscure in his poetry." This lack Mrs. Shelley does not, in any considerable degree, supply.

Nevertheless it would be churlish not to acknowledge our indebtedness to her. In two important particulars she illuminates Shelley's philosophy as set forth in *Prometheus Unbound*. Asia, "the same as Venus and Nature" is, when Prometheus is freed, "united to her husband, the emblem of the human race, in perfect and happy union." Prometheus himself is "the regenerator, who, unable to bring mankind back to primitive innocence, used knowledge as a weapon to defeat evil, by leading mankind, beyond the state wherein they are sinless through ignorance, to that in which they are virtuous through wisdom." It was Shelley's belief, she tells us, "that evil is not inherent in the system of the creation, but an accident that might be expelled. . . . Shelley believed that mankind had only to will that there should be no evil, and there would be none. . . . That man could be so perfectionized as to be able to expel evil from his own nature, and from the greater part of the creation, was the cardinal point of his system." This is the key to Shelley's ethical philosophy in *Prometheus Unbound,* and though Mrs. Shelley does not pursue its metaphysical implications, in providing so definite a point of departure she enables the reader to do so satisfactorily for himself.

II

In the latter part of the year 1818 and the early months of 1819 Shelley, in Italy, wrote the first three acts of *Prometheus Unbound*. A fourth act, creation's hymn of joy at the liberation of Prometheus, was added later in 1819, and the lyric drama, complete in four acts, was published by Ollier in 1820.

Shelley said of *Prometheus Unbound* that it was written for but five or six persons and that it was "the least imperfect" of his works. He remarked also, uncharacteristically, that the drama had cost him severe labor. These comments and a few others make it clear that he thought as well of *Prometheus Unbound* as his congenital modesty permitted; also that he cherished no illusions as to its probable favor with the reading public; in which prognosis he was correct, for in the century which followed its publication, *Prometheus Unbound* in its slow rise to fame has remained too generally unintelligible to be in any sense a popular poem. A few admirers have pronounced it one of the greatest literary works of the nineteenth century and poets have universally recognized its technical virtuosity in the manipulation of lyric forms. But there has been little success in interpreting it as a reasoned and consistent work of philosophy, despite Mary Shelley's claims in its behalf. Today the slowly growing recognition of Shelley as a thinker no less than as a lyric poet asks that *Prometheus Unbound* be more narrowly scrutinized than ever before to decipher its possible meanings.

If we may believe Mary Shelley and look to find in *Prometheus Unbound* the expression of Shelley's matured philosophy, however subtly expressed—and of the difficulties of the task she gives us warning—the method of our approach must be weighed if we are to hope for success. There are the immediate circumstances of the poem's composition to be considered: time, place, the emotional and intellectual influences recently bearing upon the poet insofar as these can be determined. We have further to weigh the symbolical character of Shelley's verse in other poems, his use of habitual images and their intellectual as well as emotional values. Last, and most formidable, we must sufficiently comprehend Shelley's culture, know the books which shaped his mind, the beliefs expressed in his earlier poems, and the trend of his intellectual development. A sufficiently difficult task this, and one not to be perfectly accomplished. Yet enough can be done to make the outlines of Shelley's philosophy as expressed in *Prometheus Unbound* emerge.

With a sense of frustration in March of 1818 Shelley left England for Italy and a life of exile. Shaken in health, robbed of his children by a hypocritical and narrow-minded society, unable longer to participate actively in political and social reform—a career which to him seemed of better worth than to write poetry so little desired by the world as was his—the four great creative years of his life, as we now perceive them to have been, were to him bleak in prospect and in their slow unfolding fraught with more unhappiness than joy. It is hard to believe that Shelley could have long been happy in this world under whatever circumstances, and perhaps Italy fostered his poetry better than any other land could have despite the ever present contrast of the beauties of nature and the tyranny and cruelty of man. In Italy were snowy mountains and azure seas. There, too, was art, in painting, sculpture, and the ruins of a noble architecture. Shelley awakened to art in Italy, and the beauty of color and form is thereafter ever present in his verse.

Prometheus Unbound was written amid the beauty of an Italian summer and autumn, but from it the enthusiasm and faith of Shelley's youth are gone. Beside *Prometheus, Queen Mab* is no more than an eloquent piece of rhetoric, but it is ardent, hopeful: the golden age is imminent; reason and the principles of the Revolutionary philosophy are soon to transform the world. The immediacy of that hope, that faith, is in *Prometheus* absent. Prometheus, the mind of man, himself—the creator of the gods, is yet by them bound to torture, is enchained by the evils of his own creation, and must endure all but endless woe before he frees himself. The ultimate despairing hope remains that he will, he must, do so. But

Utopia is no longer a matter of a few reforms and the overthrow of kings and priests. Man must change his own character; love must displace hate. *Prometheus Unbound* is the work of a poet who has ceased to be a reformer and has become a philosopher.

The full history of the development of Shelley's beliefs is too great a task to be undertaken here, nor is it essential to the present purpose. What need be known for an understanding of *Prometheus Unbound* can be briefly put, however elaborate must be the study of those beliefs as ultimately arrived at and set down in the poetic drama. Shelley's enthusiasm was, in his youth, for the radical thought of Godwin and his school, and in theories of social and political reform Shelley remained an adherent of that school to the last. Or perhaps it would be more accurate to say that a new social order based on complete justice and equality, the ideal of the Revolutionists, remained Shelley's ideal also. But the immediacy of that Utopia he no longer believed in, and in the practical means to it, as set forth in *A Philosophical View of Reform,* he became common-sensible and rather conservative.

Shelley's intellectual history, his ardent advocacy of Utopian ideals in extreme youth and his grudging surrender of his hope in their immediate realization, is in no way unusual or peculiar. It is the experience of idealistic youth the world over. The world proves more formidable, less amenable to reason, than youth can credit. With the shock of realization several consequences are characteristic. In ill-balanced minds fanaticism becomes a habit. In the weak, worldly self-interest leads often to complete apostasy; the anarchist and communist of twenty becomes at forty the typical bourgeois, hostile to all reform. But those who retain their idealism and whom disappointment does not make pessimists become the reformers who effect the slow alterations in society which we call progress. If practical expression is denied such, as in the instance of Shelley, the passion to improve the lot of man finds often an outlet in some form of art. Had Shelley remained in England one imagines that he might very well have become a disciple of Francis Place, have written reform tracts, and done a practical and useful work in the world. But it is unlikely then that he would have written *Prometheus Unbound*.

To the completion of Shelley's philosophy two other strains contribute as much as does the radical school of social reform and revolution. There was in Shelley from an early age an interest in the supernatural and the metaphysical. He dabbled in magic and summoned spirits from the vasty deep, spirits which did not come when he did call. If we may believe his statement to Hogg, at which Hogg laughed incredulously, Shelley while at Eton read and translated the works of Albertus Magnus. We need believe only that he read a part of them, acquiring thereby an early taste for Platonism. For from Hogg's report we learn that at Oxford Shelley was already imbued with Platonic ideas of preëxistence. And we learn, too, that some of the works of Thomas Taylor the Platonist were among the books read by the two friends in their Oxford days.

Shelley's intellectual development thereafter is marked by a growing Platonism. Berkeley, Spinoza, and, I believe, others such as Lord Monboddo were the means to this growth. Plato Shelley read first in English and later in the original Greek, from which as a recreation in his last years he translated parts. Nor did he, it is probable, any more than did Thomas Taylor, make any clear distinction, as would a modern scholar, between Platonism and neo-Platonism. Just which of Taylor's translations of the neo-Platonists Shelley read is not known save that, from the internal evidence in *Prometheus Unbound,* the commentary on Proclus was among them. Indeed the neo-

Platonic philosophy as set forth in Proclus, Porphyry, and Plotinus more clearly elucidates *Prometheus Unbound* than do the Platonic dialogues. Plato, though immensely stimulating and suggestive, offers no philosophic system. This the neo-Platonists do offer, and Shelley's system in *Prometheus Unbound* is akin to theirs.

There is yet a third strain to Shelley's philosophy whose importance we now for the first time fully realize, the scientific speculation of his day, which in its more imaginative and far-reaching implications is so near to the most radical thought of our time. Shelley's interest in science was genuine and in his Oxford days it was science more than literature which occupied his thoughts. In the troubled and restless years which followed he put aside scientific experimentation first for political and social agitation and later for poetical composition. But in framing his philosophic system he must needs reconcile science with metaphysics and his faith in social betterment. The task of *Prometheus Unbound* is to fuse these three diverse elements, Revolutionary social philosophy, Platonism or neo-Platonism, and scientific speculation, into a unified whole. He must reconcile materialism and idealism, physics and metaphysics, science and religion. *Prometheus Unbound* is the expression of Shelley's effort so to do. Into it he threw all the ideas in which he must believe and attempted to make them congruous, to fit them to a system. And to all this must be added as a strain of his thought or as a solvent wherein the other elements of his philosophy were blent, his acceptance of the ethics of Christ, which in his earlier days he had rejected together with the forms of institutional religion. To these latter he was throughout his life wholly averse, but the ethics of Christ became his and are embodied in his conception of Prometheus.

PROMETHEUS UNBOUND: ACT I

THE SHELLEYS on their journey to Italy traversed a bleak mountain road which was overhung with immense precipices. "The scene," Shelley writes, "is like that described in the Prometheus of Aeschylus." The allusion suggests that Shelley was then reading Aeschylus and meditating the theme of *Prometheus Unbound*. There are no earlier allusions recorded in the Shelley letters but the scheme of the poem must have been for a long time in the poet's mind. It is by far the most effective fable of the three Shelley employed in the three long poems which set forth his social philosophy. In *Queen Mab* the mechanism is slight and of little interest. The poem is an eloquent indictment of the evils of the world as it now is and a picture of the golden age to be. But speaker and audience have in themselves no dramatic or story value. In the *Revolt of Islam* there is too much story rather than too little. The social philosophy is dispersed in an action too wild and copious, which is at the same time monotonous and fatiguing. In the first three acts of *Prometheus Unbound* there is action sufficient for the poem's philosophic purpose, a fable which lends itself ideally to symbolic treatment.

An action so laden with philosophic meanings, in which the characters are themselves symbolic, cannot have been quickly improvised; but speculation as to the date of its inception is necessarily guesswork. A plausible story could be spun that Shelley in 1816 had the theme in mind and that Byron got the idea for his Prometheus from conversations with Shelley who read and translated the Prometheus of Aeschylus for him. Such a surmise is based on the belief that Byron would not unprompted have thought of the theme. And in support, is the use, in *Manfred,* of the anecdote of Iamblichus and the two youthful gods of love evoked from the fountain, an anecdote to be found in Taylor's *Proclus,* which is the evident source of much of the symbolism in *Prometheus Unbound.* It is my guess that Byron got the episode from Shelley. But this is admittedly only conjecture. More certain it is that the consistency with which Shelley's recondite philosophy was in *Prometheus Unbound* worked out and dramatized with a subtle symbolism, asked not only the arduous months which Shelley devoted to the writing but months or years of germination also.

The essential theme of the Prometheus fable, that of the fire-bringer befriending men and defying the gods, was one to call forth in Shelley a sympathetic response. Lucretius had lauded the Titan in the epic which Shelley admired when a boy in Eton; it was then, conceivably, that the germ of *Prometheus Unbound* took root to flower a decade after. For the story as Shelley employs it, the *Prometheus Bound* of Aeschylus is the apparent source, though there are many allusions to Prometheus elsewhere in ancient literature. In Aeschylus, Prometheus is heroic in his defiance of Jupiter and remains in the course of the play firm not to betray the secret which threatens the reign of Jupiter. In the sequel, the lost play of Aeschylus, *Prometheus Unbound,* Prometheus surrenders to Jupiter and is freed from his torment. With this reading Shelley's *Prometheus Unbound* has little in common.

In the *Prometheus Unbound* of Shelley the reader's knowledge of Aeschylus is assumed to explain the marriage of Jupiter and Thetis; and Jupiter's overthrow by Demogorgon, which by that marriage he thought to avert, is an echo of the ancient prophecy. Yet the story here is no more than a framework upon which Shelley hangs his own philosophy and the reader is rather less perplexed by the fable if ignorant of the Aeschylean version. In Shelley's allegory it is the mind of man which creates and which destroys Jupiter. Demogorgon, personification of Fate or Necessity, is the tool. And it is the mind of man, personified in Prometheus, which Shelley glorifies in its passionate endurance of all the torture which Jupiter can heap upon it. In his forgiveness of Jupiter, Prometheus by his compassion destroys the evil which hatred and defiance could not destroy. Philosophical and ethical meanings foreign to Greek thought clothe the fable in a new dress. The ethics of Christ is fused with the metaphysics of Plato.

Yet the dramatic situation at the outset and the stage properties and characters are Aeschylean. Echoes of the Greek original are evident throughout the opening scene. Prometheus the Titan, the friend and instructor of mankind, is suffering his age-long torture chained to a bleak precipice in the Indian Caucasus. In a long and superb passage of blank verse he expresses his deathless defiance of Jupiter, prophesies the hour which shall drag the tyrant from his throne, and recalls the curse he had long ago passed upon Jupiter, a curse which all creation cherishes but dare not repeat. Philosophic difficulties are apparent at the outset, in the second line to be exact:

> Monarch of Gods, and Daemons, and all Spirits
> But One . . .

The Daemons are of the Platonic and neo-Platonic theology, spirits somewhat lower in the heavenly hierarchy than the Gods. But who is the One whom, only, Jupiter cannot subdue?[1]

The One in neo-Platonic and Platonic terminology is God. But so to define the term is inexact. The One is the ineffable aspect, the abstract all-perfect source of all things, the hypostasis which is truth, beauty, perfection. In the theology of

---

[1] In the unique manuscript of the poem "one" is seemingly not capitalized. Whether, then, Shelley here means the One of neo-Platonic thought, or whether Prometheus, is not certain. But if my later argument is sound, that Prometheus is himself to be identified with the One, the point is immaterial.

Plotinus the One is the well-spring of the universe. He likens it to a point or center around which revolve the other two hypostases of divinity: the intellectual or thought-creative aspect, and the emotional-creative aspect which realizes in material forms the creations of divine thought. In the words of Prometheus, Jupiter has subdued to his sway all but the One, the Ineffable, who is love, truth, perfection. The One is the eternal God whereas Jupiter is a lesser and temporal God. The metaphysics of this seeming paradox becomes clear as the poem unfolds.

Of all created things Prometheus alone resists the will of Jupiter for,

> Whilst me, who am thy foe, eyeless in hate,
> Hast thou made reign and triumph, to thy scorn,
> O'er mine own misery and thy vain revenge. . . .

It is not, then, quite true that Jupiter is monarch over all but the One. He is not wholly master of Prometheus himself who, though subjected to torture and a captive, is yet master of his soul and his defiance. Therein is the suggestion that Prometheus to some degree shares the divinity of the One, that in the obduracy of his will, his independence of mind, he is superior to Jupiter. Dramatically the scene predicts the conflict of tyrant and rebel and the protagonist's ultimate triumph. Dramatically, also, the repetition of the curse is exposition which reveals incidents prior to the action and which serves to contrast the mood of hate in which the curse was uttered and the mood of sorrowing pity in which it is recalled.

> . . . I speak in grief,
> Not exultation, for I hate no more,
> As then, ere misery made me wise.

Mrs. Shelley's notes on Prometheus explain Shelley's belief "that evil is not inherent in the system of the creation but an

accident that might be expelled. . . . Shelley believed that
mankind had only to will that there should be no evil and
there would be none." Again she speaks of "Humanity, typ-
ified in Prometheus," and of Prometheus as the "Benefactor
of Mankind." This seeming paradox authentically conveys
Shelley's conception as it is unfolded in the course of the
drama. Dramatically Prometheus is the liberator of humanity
from the tyranny of Jupiter; yet Prometheus is also humanity
itself. Humanity, as the drama expounds the role of Prometheus, creates the evil which it suffers and ultimately destroys
that evil, personified by the Jupiter of its creation, thus finding
freedom and happiness. The duality of the conception is
perhaps more intelligible if Prometheus is thought of as a
personification of the racial will of mankind, its power to endure and defy its own evil creation, a kind of deathless super-
soul greater than its mortal constituents. Prometheus so
conceived resembles the Platonic personifications of earth,
moon, and the heavenly bodies, which are worshiped as Gods.
Or he may be thought of as the archetypal idea of Humanity,
the reality of the ideal world which manifests itself imperfectly
in the material world, the world which evolves in the effort to
realize the archetypal pattern of perfection.

Such a conception is Platonistic and has, too, evolutionary
implications. The most interesting and alien element assim-
ilated to this philosophy is, however, the definitely Christian
concept of the conquest of evil through forgiveness. The opening monologue in *Prometheus Unbound,* which expresses the
defiance and unshaken fortitude of Prometheus, ends with his
expression of pity for his enemy. This, as the ensuing action
reveals, is the prelude to Jupiter's overthrow. Shelley in this
philosophy is in accord with the ethics of Christ. Prometheus
in ceasing to hate evil overcomes evil.

In accord with the ethics of Christ but unalterably hostile

to ecclesiasticism, to institutional religion and the God whom it perpetuates, whether Christian or pagan, if cruel, is the picture of human woe and abject worship:

> . . . regard this Earth
> Made multitudinous with thy slaves, whom thou
> Requitest for knee-worship, prayer, and praise,
> And toil, and hecatombs of broken hearts,
> With fear and self-contempt. . . .

The self-contempt, abasement, and false shame fostered by religion Shelley repeatedly execrates. It is an idea which Godwin too had expressed. Shelley's ardent adoption of it can hardly have been born of his own spiritual experience, for there is no evidence that he was himself ever much of a conventional believer or that his conversion to scepticism was a profound spiritual struggle. Rather he saw in religion the foe to the natural life, the happy life, of man. And in the surrender to religious authority was implicit the surrender both of happiness and independence of mind. To the French Revolutionary thinkers, to Godwin, and to Shelley the two institutions which most enslave mankind are the church and the state. Of the two Shelley hates the church the more, because it is the more insidious; in its subtle demoralization of the mind, the more evil.

Two or three allusions of scientific import are to be noted in the opening monologue uttered by Prometheus: the reference to the "crawling glacier," to the "genii of the storm," and

> Thou serenest Air
> Through which the Sun walks burning without beams!

These details I have elsewhere explained in full.[1a] It is important only to note that the scientific imagery early appears and assumes even greater importance in the progress of the

[1a] *A Newton Among Poets*, p. 152.

drama. The lyrics which follow the monologue of Prometheus
are full of it. The voice from the mountains speaks:

> Thrice three hundred thousand years
> O'er the earthquake's couch we stood;[2]

Again, the Voice from the Springs:

> Thunderbolts had parched our water[3]

And the Third Voice, from the Air:

> I had clothed, since Earth uprose,
> Its wastes in colours not their own![4]

All are scientific in their import and suggest the range and
currency of Shelley's scientific knowledge.

Voices from the four elements and of Earth, mother of all,
repeat the dread effect of the curse which Prometheus passed
upon his enemy but dare not repeat the words. Prometheus
addresses the Earth in a passage of a few lines upon which it
is needful to pause, for they touch closely ideas of fundamental
importance to Shelley's philosophy.

> Mother, thy sons and thou
> Scorn him, without whose all-enduring will
> Beneath the fierce omnipotence of Jove,
> Both they and thou had vanished, like thin mist
> Unrolled on the morning wind!

And in his first soliloquy Prometheus, in addressing Jupiter,
says,

> O Mighty God!
> Almighty, had I deigned to share the shame
> Of thine ill tyranny . . .

The Titan in his defiance of Jupiter has, it is clear, prevented
the destruction of the Earth and the sons of earth. But pre-

---

[2] *Ibid.*, p. 180. [3] *Ibid.*, p. 137. [4] *Ibid.*, p. 153.

cisely how can this be? The answer involves a brief exposition of Shelley's Platonic philosophy.

The use here of the term "Platonic" must be apologized for. It is a term of convenience, and by it is meant not only the philosophy which Shelley learned from Plato but also that from the neo-Platonists. Modern scholars, such as Jowett, make a sharp division between the two and deny to Plato those mystical interpretations to be found in the words of Plotinus, Proclus, Porphyry, and Iamblichus. Thomas Taylor the Platonist, with whose work Shelley was in some degree familiar, makes no such distinction. Nor is it evident that Shelley does so. Plato and the interpreters of Plato, I believe, formed for him one body of metaphysical and, frequently, mystical doctrine from which he took whatever he desired. In interpreting *Prometheus Unbound* it is profitable, therefore, to leave aside all question of the purity of the Platonic doctrine and to bring to bear, whatever their source, those philosophic ideas which aid in making the poem intelligible. By "Platonic" is meant, then, those ideas which originate in Plato or are ascribed to him, it may be inaccurately, by his followers the neo-Platonists.

How, then, does the will of the Titan, exerted against the cruel purpose of Jupiter, prevent the destruction of the material world?

In the philosophy of Plotinus matter is described as all but non-being. It is the very verge, the vanishing point, of created things, the farthest from that center of reality which is God in whom everything exists. The aspects of God are threefold: first, the mysterious well-spring of force of which nothing can be postulated except that it supremely is and is synonymous with perfect truth, beauty, and reality; second, the intellectual aspect or "hypostasis" in which exist all those ideas which the third, or creative, hypostasis realizes in the sensible universe.

The creative phase or hypostasis materializes the ideas of deity, but the materializations are less "real"—are, that is, less permament and fixed—than the ideas of which they are approximations. Essential true existence lies, therefore, in thought, than which matter is less perfectly "real."

The universe may be said to exist in the brain of God, but if the lines in *Prometheus Unbound* are to be read as I interpret them and it is only the will of Prometheus which prevents the earth and the sons of earth from vanishing, then Prometheus in Shelley's conception is God or a part of God, sharing the intellection which is the true reality and in the patterns of which all material things are cast. That some such idea is at the root of Shelley's "system" will more completely appear as the philosophy of the poem unfolds. Meanwhile it should be borne in mind and the relation of it to Shelley's conception of Asia considered.

The allusion to Asia is in Prometheus' invocation of Mother Earth after the voices of the elements have refused his request that they repeat the curse passed upon Jupiter:

> . . . Mother, thy sons and thou
> Scorn him, without whose all-enduring will
> Beneath the fierce omnipotence of Jove,
> Both they and thou had vanished like thin mist
> Unrolled on the morning wind. Know ye not me,
> The Titan? He who made his agony
> The barrier to your else all-conquering foe?
> O, rock-embosomed lawns and snow-fed streams,
> Now seen athwart frore vapors, deep below,
> Through whose o'ershadowing woods I wandered once
> With Asia, drinking life from her loved eyes;

Mrs. Shelley's notes explain that "Asia, one of the Oceanides, is the wife of Prometheus—she was, according to other mythological interpretations, the same as Venus and Nature." The imprisonment of Prometheus signalizes his separation from

the life-giving forces of nature, the life which he has drunk
from her eyes. This "life," as other passages indicate and as I
have shown elsewhere at length, is also "love," and, in a second aspect, electricity or force.[5] The spirit of man languishes
because he is divorced from the natural life. He is deprived
of life, love, and energy in the degree once his. The lines are
clearly reminiscent of the natural man theory of Rousseau
and others, a theory which Shelley endeavors to reconcile with
other tenets, scientific and Platonic, in his philosophy. With
the overthrow of Jupiter, mankind, as personified in Prometheus, is to be restored to its prior estate and live in harmony
with nature.

Prometheus demands of Earth herself the curse which
none dare repeat. To which the Earth replies:

> How canst thou hear
> Who knowest not the language of the dead?

Shelley's meaning here and in some subsequent passages of
similar tenor is not easy. How indeed can there be a language
of these as yet untenanted shades? That the experience of
mortality is not that of immortality is clear enough, for the
life of the "dead," if they are conscious, is twofold, in being
and remembrance, whereas the life of immortals is but one.
Yet there is a seeming juggling of the terms life and death
suggestive of the lines in *The Sensitive Plant:*

> To own that death itself must be
> Like all the rest, a mockery.

> —ll. 127-28.

The Earth's speech slightly prior to this ambiguous passage
contains the lines:

> Subtle thou art and good; and though the Gods
> Hear not this voice, yet thou art more than God,
> Being wise and kind:

[5] *Ibid.,* pp. 132, 185.

God, in the words of Earth, must mean Jupiter, "Heaven's fell King." The moral greatness of Prometheus and his wisdom make him superior to the reigning deity in all save force, which force is denied to Prometheus in his separation from Asia. Later passages suggest that in the reign of Jupiter the force resident in nature has been usurped by him and becomes in his hands not love but hate. But it suffices here to note that in this speech of Earth's the ultimate triumph of moral goodness is forecast.

In a long passage the Earth describes the birth of Prometheus.

> When thou didst from her bosom, like a beam
> From sunrise, leap—a spirit of keen joy!
> And at thy voice her pining sons uplifted
> Their prostrate brows from the polluting dust
> And our almighty Tyrant with fierce dread
> Grew pale. . . .

The lines are difficult to reconcile with the ancient myth in which Prometheus, a Titan, is of the older gods before their overthrow by Jupiter; indeed Prometheus aided Jupiter in his rebellion. Nor is it possible I think to reconcile with it the statement in the poem that Prometheus gave Jupiter all he has, that Jupiter is indeed the creation of Prometheus. The only way in which consistency can be secured is to assume that the lines

> . . . thou didst from her bosom, like a cloud
> Of glory, arise,

refer not to the birth of Prometheus but to an incarnation of his spirit, his separation from Mother Earth. It is somewhat easier, I think, to convict Shelley in this instance of a slight inconsistency.

The Earth then describes the evils which befell mankind when, Prometheus being chained, famine and plague smote them and the beneficent gifts of nature were poisoned at their spring.

> . . . the thin air, my breath, was stained
> With the contagion of a mother's hate.

Prometheus thereupon repeats his demand that his curse be spoken. The Earth no longer refuses but evokes the Phantasm of Jupiter for that purpose, the nature of which Phantasm the Earth explains in lines of great interest but of considerable philosophic difficulty. The peculiarities of the passage are such that the first half should be recalled in its entirety:

> . . . . Ere Babylon was dust,
> The Magus Zoroaster, my dead child,
> Met his own image walking in the garden.
> That apparition, sole of men, he saw.
> For know there are two worlds of life and death:
> One that which thou beholdest; but the other
> Is underneath the grave, where do inhabit
> The shadows of all forms that think and live,
> Till death unite them, and they part no more;
> Dreams and the light imaginings of men,
> And all that faith creates or love desires,
> Terrible, strange, sublime, and beauteous shapes.
> There thou art, and dost hang, a writhing shade,
> 'Mid whirlwind-shaken mountains; all the gods
> Are there, and all the powers of nameless worlds.

Confusion existed in antiquity among historians and philosophers as to the identity of Zoroaster and in Shelley's day it was believed (*e. g.* Rees' *Cyclopedia*) that there were two Zoroasters, one the Persian religious leader, the other a Bactryan wizard of some indeterminate but earlier time. The cause of this confusion, it may be surmised, was the occultism of the Magi of the time immediately after that of the true Zoroaster and their corruption of his tenets. Neo-Platonistic writers early in the Christian era, deriving their theology in

part from Oriental doctrines, apparently took over from Zoroastrianism some of its mystical beliefs, and perpetuated leg-
ends, more or less apocryphal, of the supposed originator of
these beliefs. I believe it is from some, as yet unidentified,
neo-Platonic source that Shelley cites the anecdote of Zoroaster
meeting his image in the garden.

That his phrasing implies some specific and recorded incident, whether or no of any authenticity, is, I think, clear.
What Shelley's Oriental reading was aside from the works of
Sir William Jones is not known, though the writers of antiquity would have taught him somewhat, and Plutarch, whose
works Shelley knew, mentions Zoroaster and characterizes him
as a Mage. Shelley's mysticism has, indeed, its resemblances
to true Zoroastrianism in its characteristic contrasts of light
and darkness which in Zoroastrianism denote the powers of
good and evil, Ormuzd and Ahriman. It is characteristic also
of the teachings of Zoroaster that evil is something alien to the
scheme of Ormuzd, an intrusion for which he is not responsible. Shelley's effort in *Prometheus Unbound* to explain
evil as not inevitable or enduring is analogous.

The effort to trace Shelley's eclectic mysticism to specific
sources is usually, however, a thankless task, for his philosophy
is variously derived. Its chief source, whether Platonism or
neo-Platonism, is moreover in itself a mixed stream of many
elements, some Greek, some Oriental. I shall content myself
with citing analogies to Shelley's philosophy wherever found
and employ these in the interpretation of his "system," which
I take to be, in its synthesis, his own, similar as it is on one
side or another to the various philosophies and mythologies
which supplied him with suggestions.

The Magus Zoroaster of Shelley's phrase may, then, be
Zoroaster the wise man of philosophic fame or the wizard
Zoroaster. In either case the episode of meeting his own

image is probably apocryphal, although the experience is a not uncommon psychical phenomenon. Shelley himself encountered his own image only a few days before his death, though the experience was apparently somnambulistic.[6] Common superstition holds it to be prophetic of approaching death.

It is Shelley's inferences and explanations which make the passage of so great interest in his philosophy. What can be the nature of this "image," suggestive both of the "astral body" of Theosophy and of the shades which, in classical belief, inhabited the underworld after death. Neither in classical mythology nor in Theosophy, apparently, does the explanation wholly lie. In Platonism and in folk-lore are to be found truer analogies, and in Porphyry, as cited by Proclus, the most explicit source that I have been able to find.[7]

Folk beliefs that linger in fairy tales often divorce the worldly existence from the true existence of giant or wizard. Thus the hero destroys his enemy in many guises but can never wholly end him until he discovers and destroys the soul which resides apart, hidden perhaps in an egg in the body of a duck which swims in a well at the other end of the earth.[8] The earthly body is a transient thing in this belief and true existence is elsewhere. So too, in Theosophy, one of the soul's "vehicles," the physical body, is enclosed within another, the astral body. In trance the astral body may divorce itself from the physical body and wander at will. It survives the physical body for a time, but eventually also dies, whereupon the real individuality or soul resides in its mental body, which is indestructible.

[6] For this and the instance of Shelley's "double" seen in the garden by Jane Williams and Trelawny see Edward Dowden, *Life of Shelley*, 2 vols. (1886), II, 515-16.

[7] Quotation follows *infra*.

[8] See Sir James George Frazer, *The Golden Bough: Balder the Beautiful*, in 2 vols. (London, Macmillan and Company, Ltd., 1913), II, 109, 115, 119.

A triune conception of the human soul similar to that of the One is to be found in Plotinus, who argues that the soul of man has three phases or hypostases: the intellective soul, which knows through intuition and is ever seeking its home in God; the reasoning soul, which by the slow processes of logic arrives at those truths which the intellective soul apprehends by intuition; and the unreasoning soul which is the principle of animal life. Of these souls, or phases of the soul, only the first is eternal. The others perish as does the body.

A similar and more complicated doctrine is taught by Porphyry and it is from this, as cited by Proclus, that I have derived the most intelligible explanation of the soul residing as a shadow in Hades during the mortal existence of its earthly counterpart. One passage I shall cite as most germane to the immediate theme. It is difficult reading, either because the original is so or because Thomas Taylor, the translator, is even more than usually obscure. It is not, however, when considered in the light of a modern philosophy similar to it but more intelligible, Theosophy, unprofitable; and its relation to Shelley's lines can be established.

As the soul's residence on the earth, (says he) does not consist in being conversant in the earth, as bodies, but in presiding over bodies situated on the earth: so likewise the soul is said to be in Hades, when she presides over her image, which has a nature accommodated to place, but then obtains a subsistence in darkness. Hence if Hades is a subterranean dark place, the soul though not separated from being, dwells in this case in Hades, attracting to herself her image. For the spirit which she had collected from the spheres, attends her in her departure from a solid body. But from her affection towards body, reason having a partial object, according to which, she obtained a habitude towards a body of this kind, while she lived; from this propense affection, a form of the phantasy is impressed on the spirit, and so she attracts the image. But she is said to be in Hades, because she obtains a spirit of a formless and dark nature: and since a heavy and humid spirit, extends to subterranean places, on this account also the soul is said to dwell under the earth; not because her essence passes from place to place, and subsists in place, but because it receives the habits of bodies endued with a natural inclination to local transitions, and the possession of place. And bodies of this kind indeed, receive the soul, according to aptitudes, from a certain disposition towards her nature. For according to her particular disposition, she finds a body defined, correspondent to her order and properties. Hence when the soul is in a more pure condition of being, a body is natural to her, approximating very nearly to that which is immaterial; such as an etherial body. But when she proceeds from reason to the object of imagination, she naturally forms a solar-form body; and when effeminated and captivated with the love of forms, she is united with a lunar-form body. Lastly, when she falls into bodies composed from humid vapours, a perfect ignorance of being succeeds, and darkness and infancy. And indeed in her egress from body, when she retains a spirit disturbed by a humid evaporation, she attracts a shade, and is weighed down; a spirit of this kind, endeavoring to dwell naturally in the bottom of the earth, unless some other cause draws it into a contrary place. As therefore when surrounded with this terrene shell, it is necessary she should reside on the earth; so likewise when she attracts a humid spirit, it is necessary she should be surrounded with the image. But she attracts moisture, when she continually studies to be present with a nature, whose operation consists in moisture, and is mostly subterranean. But when she endeavors to depart from nature, she becomes a dry splendor, without a shadow, and without a cloud: for humidity constitutes a cloud in the air; but dryness produces from vapour, a dry splendor.[9]

From this it appears that the soul in its earthly incarnation takes to itself a humid dress or vehicle in which resides a spirit that is not the true soul at all, this latter being resident in the realm of intellective being. The soul presides over its earthly "vehicle" and over that untenanted "vehicle" which awaits the

[9] Thomas Taylor, *The Philosophical and Mathematical Commentaries of Proclus,* 2 vols. (London, 1792), II, 271, note, quoting from Porphyry in Senten. 32, p. 232.

spirit in the lower world until the decease of the earthly body. The "shadows of all forms that think and live" are the vehicles prepared for them, having no life of their own until inhabited by the spirits of the dead. Nor is this second existence or incarnation any more "real" than is earthly existence. From it ultimately the soul wholly withdraws to its true realm, that of mental existence, having in its incarnations acquired the experience it desired or which was demanded of it.

For those of simple mind there are, in this explanation of Proclus, over-many souls, spirits, bodies, and vehicles all belonging to the one individual. Yet the belief is fundamentally like that of Theosophy which, though difficult, is lucidly set forth to some such effect as this: The individual soul exists successively on many planes of being, the lowest of which is the animal, on which plane its existence is three-fold: physical, which perishes with death; astral, which survives the physical body but ultimately is destroyed; mental, which is real and imperishable and in which form the soul resides for an indeterminate time after the destruction of the astral body, before it is obliged to endure another earthly incarnation. Ultimately in its evolutionary history the soul no longer need be reincarnated in earthly form but pursues its course on successively higher planes of being—these of indefinite number of which the Theosophists identify, I believe, seven. At long last the soul is again wholly absorbed in the divine—the Nirvana of Indian desire.

In a fashion recognizably Platonistic Shelley pursues the implications of this theme. If the image which resides in Hades is the creation of intellection, as in Platonic theology all worldly existences and the unrealities of matter are, it follows intelligibly enough that all the thoughts, imaginings, and desires of men have likewise their images. Thought creates; and though the thing created is less real than the thought itself, it has a kind of existence. So Shelley seems to declare in the passage under discussion. In *Adonais* the same idea is expressed. The creations of the dead poet, having been made alive by his thought, mourn their creator's death:

> All he had loved, and moulded into thought,
> From shape, and hue, and odor, and sweet sound,
> Lamented Adonais.
> —XIV, ll. 118-20.

The underworld is peopled, then, by images, shadows of all the actualities of the world which are the product of divine intellection; and shadows, also, of human intellection—the dreams, imaginings, and desires of men. After death the spirits of which these are the shadows are incorporated with them in the future existence. It is a curious mythology, whose implications Shelley does not pursue, contenting himself in the present instance by employing this machinery to recall the curse passed by Prometheus upon Jupiter. It is the phantasm of Jupiter, this empty image in the lower world, which, though non-existent in itself, is made to speak.

What conception Shelley holds of this world of the dead can be gathered only from his words. The phantasm speaks:

> . . . What unaccustomed sounds
> Are hovering on my lips, unlike the voice
> With which our pallid race hold ghastly talk
> In darkness?

From this it would seem that some degree of life animates the "pallid race" of shadows even though

> . . . the revenge
> Of the Supreme may sweep through vacant shades
> As rainy wind through the abandoned gate
> Of a fallen palace.

The critic at this point ardently wishes that Shelley had composed, as he intended, that gloss upon *Prometheus Unbound* which would have elucidated its mysteries. If Shelley has, in the lines I have cited, propounded a paradox, I fear it must so be left.

Prometheus summons the "phantasm of Jupiter" to arise, whereupon speak for the first time, Ione and Panthea, the sisters of Asia who bring comfort to Prometheus,

> Near whom, for our sweet sister's sake,
> Ever thus we watch and wake.

Ione and Panthea play their parts in the symbolism of the drama and their functions are differentiated. But it will be best to consider them at a later time in conjunction with Asia and when the part which they play as go-betweens ministering to both Asia and Prometheus is more evident. It may be pertinent to note here only that Ione first perceives the phantasm, although she says

> My wings are folded o'er mine ears;
> My wings are crossèd o'er mine eyes;

The Earth bids the mountains and woods listen to the words of the phantasm.

> Prophetic caves, and isle-surrounding streams,
> Rejoice to hear what yet ye dare not speak.

The curse of Prometheus, the ills which, in his defiance, he calls upon Jupiter to bring down upon him and upon mankind are prophecies of the event. These evils and more Jupiter has created. Prometheus wishes his enemy to heap up his "fruitless crimes" so that destruction will be inevitable, the fall catastrophic and eternal. It is an eloquent passage, but its chief philosophic significance resides in the lines:

> Thou art omnipotent.
> O'er all things but thyself I gave thee power,
> And my own will.

Jupiter, then, is the creation of Prometheus, omnipotent but for lack of self-mastery and strength to crush the will of man. For it was evident from the earlier discussion and from Mrs. Shelley's statement that Prometheus is the common mind or will of man, the over-soul, the personification of mankind as a whole, summing in himself the lives of individual men but greater than the sum of the parts of which he is constituted.

It is a familiar notion in the literature of the French revolutionary philosophy that the gods are made by man in the likeness of himself. As put by Voltaire, "God made man in his own image and man returned the compliment." Yet there remains in Prometheus, creator of Jupiter, something recalcitrant and unsubdued which is superior to the God he has made. This is the creative will, which, in man, as in the One of the theology of Platonism, is prior to and greater than all its works. Superior though it be to its creations it is nevertheless subject to them in the same way that a man is subject to the thoughts which have been his. These constitute his mental history and tradition, just as the creations of deity constitute the history and tradition of its thought; are indeed its thought materialized. Thought evolves, and the forms of life, the phenomena of the material world, likewise evolve in an ever lengthening chain which is continuous and unbroken. The past cannot be destroyed. It can at best be forgiven.

Shelley as a youth was of the school of radicals who looked upon history as little more than the record of human error. Their faith, their entire interest, lay in the future. Hence their enthusiasm, their passion for reform, and their impatience of the past. Hence, too, their disillusionment, when they found that the past lay like a dead hand upon men. Neither reason nor imagination sufficed to free mankind from the heritage of its own errors. So Shelley came to see, to the enrichment of his philosophic thought. Jupiter is man's creation, but man cannot merely unthink him. Jupiter is because he has been. He lives in fear and hate just as a past sin lives in remorse. As the sin is forgiven it ceases to plague and may be forgotten. As Jupiter is forgiven, not hated, his power drops from him and he too may be forgotten. This, I take it, is the psychological truth which underlies the struggle of Prometheus with his own creation, Jupiter. Shelley's imprecations elsewhere upon remorse are a confirmation of this view.

Shelley's struggle in the development of his philosophy is, of necessity, with the ideology of his time. The heritage of the French Revolutionary philosophies which emancipated him from the timid and base beliefs of the Napoleonic reactionary era laid too its inevitable fetters upon him. Disrespect for, lack of interest in and understanding of, the past was one of its limitations, one which he outgrew and in the struggle learned much. Not with all of the accepted beliefs of this school was he so successful. The golden age, the state of nature, man's innocence and happiness prior to the "fall"—however this last is conceived—all this belief in a mythical Eden is not easily reconcilable with a belief in the evolution of man from a lower form to a higher. Yet myth and the philosophy of Rousseau predicate a golden age of some remote and legendary past. Shelley perforce accepted it and endeavored to find a place for it in his scheme, to reconcile it with the problem of sin and sin's advent in the world. Why then did man, if happy once, create Jupiter to his own enslavement? This problem is not so satisfactorily solved, I think, as is that of Jupiter's destruction, once he is created, through forgiveness. It is the old problem of the justification of evil in a world created by an all-good, all-powerful Providence. If Shelley does not solve it satisfactorily, it yet may be said that he has for company all the idealistic philosophers of record. But to return to the next incident of the drama.

The God whom Prometheus has endowed with power was, in times long past, cursed by Prometheus. Now the image or phantasm of Jupiter, that empty shade which yet speaks the "incommunicable language of the dead," repeats the curse. Thereat the Titan speaks:

> It doth repent me: words are quick and vain;
> Grief for awhile is blind, and so was mine.
> I wish no living thing to suffer pain.

It is these words which mark the overthrow of Jupiter. The event now is sure and the ensuing incidents prepare the dramatic catastrophe. Yet the triumph of love over hatred which Prometheus expresses in his words is thought by the Earth to mark his surrender to Jupiter.

> Misery, Oh, misery to me,
> That Jove at length should vanquish thee!

And it seems for the moment that the Earth's lament is warranted, for the cruelty of Jupiter is at once poured in even greater measure than before upon Prometheus.

The Furies stream up from hell to work the horrid will of Jupiter. It is Ione who first perceives and describes them, Panthea who explains what they are. Ione asks

> Are they now led from the thin dead
> On new pangs to be fed?

Shelley's conception here is derived apparently from mixed neo-Platonic and magical sources. These "thought executing ministers of Jove," the product of his "mis-creating brain," are akin to

> Dreams and the light imaginings of men,
> And all that faith creates, or love desires,
> Terrible, strange, sublime, and beauteous shapes.

Creations of thought and passion, these ministers of Jove dwell in the world

> . . . where do inhabit
> The shadows of all forms that think and live.

They live because all that is thought and desired assumes a phantom existence which, apparently, may be embodied in more material forms.

The materialization of the Furies springs from their desire

> On new pangs to be fed.

They are

> Jove's tempest-walking hounds,
> Whom he gluts with groans and blood.

Denied their prey through the command of Mercury, the Furies cry,

> Oh, mercy! mercy!
> We die with our desire: drive us not back!

And again, later, when the Furies are loosed to work their will upon Prometheus, one exclaims

> So from our victim's destined agony
> The shade which is our form invests us round;
> Else are we shapeless as our mother Night.

That thoughts and desires achieve form and materiality as their purpose is realized is of a piece with the Platonic philosophy that all creative thought seeks material expression. The thought of God is reflected in the material universe which the third aspect of divinity, the Demi-urge, shapes at its instigation. The thought and passion of Jupiter, therefore, though feebler than that of the One, must likewise seek realization, which is found in the present instance in the action of the Furies. Their forms are moulded from the pain and blood of their victims, a conception analogous to that which prompted animal sacrifices to demons.

It was held that these sacrifices to the demons were more acceptable than exhalations from other things, because that in the fumes there were more vivid traces of the living soul, and so a greater relationship. Hence in invocations to the demons and to the manes or shades of the dead, victims were immolated in order that a nourishing exhalation might be obtained from the flowing blood.[10]

Practises of black magic are also akin, the exhalations from a blood-filled vessel serving, when accompanied by the proper incantations, to provide a medium for the materialization of the evil spirit invoked. The spirit is thus given form visible to the magician. In the practises of spiritualism likewise, the ectoplasm drawn from the body of the medium serves a similar purpose, shaping itself to the thought forms existing in the mind of the medium or the questioner. Or so, presumably, if the phenomena are authentic, the materializing medium is employed. Its resemblance, in any case, to the materializations accredited to sacrificial blood offerings and the practises of black magic is noteworthy. Shelley's materialization of the Furies is therefore not so unintelligible and far-fetched as at first sight it seems, and the suggestion for it may have come from any of several sources.

The words of Mercury to Prometheus,

> . . . there is a secret known
> To thee, and to none else of living things,
> Which may transfer the sceptre of wide Heaven,
> The fear of which perplexes the Supreme.

refer to the myth which Aeschylus employs. From the marriage of Zeus to Thetis is to come a son, Achilles, greater than his father, who is to overthrow him. The use which Shelley makes of this legend is merely to provide a framework for the dramatic narrative. As later appears it is no demigod or

---

[10] *The Egyptian Mysteries* by Iamblichos, translated anew and annotated by Alexander Wilder, M.D., F.A.S. (American School of Metaphysics, Greenwich, Conn., 1915), p. 198, footnote.

earthly warrior who is to unseat Jupiter but Demogorgon.
Mercury's appeal serves to reveal the Titan's unswerving will.
That Prometheus repents of his curse implies no yielding to
Jupiter.

> Submission, thou dost know I cannot try:
> For what submission but that fatal word,
> The death-seal of mankind's captivity,
>
> .   .   .   .
>
> . . . would he accept,
> Or could I yield?

That mankind, or the will of man personified in Prometheus,
refuses allegiance to the god of its creating is the sole hope of
ultimate deliverance.

Prometheus, in his refusal to yield, repeats his earlier
words, that he has endowed Jupiter with power:

> . . . I gave all
> He has . . .
>
> —l. 382.

And in return Jupiter has enchained Prometheus, for

> . . . Evil minds
> Change good to their own nature.
> —ll. 380-81.

The philosophical perplexity here lies in Shelley's conception
of Jupiter who, though the creation of man's will (Prometheus), and endowed with good, perverts good to evil and
enslaves man. The solution to this difficulty is not explicit in
Shelley's words and must be inferred. He was, I take it,
thinking of the past of man's theology, and the various concepts of God which are expressed in religions old and new.
The gods of these differ as men's ideals have differed in the
evolution of the race. Each god in his day expressed the ideals
of his worshipers, was the personification of the best they

knew: a god of vengeance or retaliation, a god of war and animal sacrifice, or a fatherly and benignant god. Whatever his virtues once, these in time become evils, for the ideas which harden into ecclesiastical systems are not easily changed. They lie a dead weight on future generations. So Shelley believed, as is evident in his enduring hatred of ecclesiasticism. In this he is true to his Revolutionary origins and but echoes the words of Voltaire, Paine, and Godwin.

With this interpretation the philosophical paradox in Shelley's words is satisfactorily solved. Man is the victim of his past, not only of his evil deeds but of his best ideals, for these too became inadequate. They enslave and restrict:

> Evil minds
> Change good to their own nature.

The evil in Jupiter is that he persists, that he survives the need of his creation yet is not easily destroyed. I believe this is intelligible and true of the race as of the individual. The past must slowly be erased, must indeed be forgiven, as Prometheus forgives Jupiter. But Shelley's philosophy implies faith in an evolving universe, both physical and moral, and the reconciliation of such a faith with a belief in a prior golden age we have yet to make, if we can, in our interpretation of the symbols Shelley employs in subsequent passages.

Of dramatic necessity *Prometheus Unbound* depicts that moment in the conflict of Prometheus and Jupiter in which the balance turns and the catastrophe is forecast. The time, though indefinite, must be short, the action closely linked and urgent. Yet it is evident that Shelley's Utopian faith in the golden age to be is no longer belief in sudden revolution. Prometheus is confident only that some day the evil reign of Jupiter will end and Justice triumph. All but infinite the time may be before this happy event. The mind

> Perchance . . . has not numbered the slow years
> Which thou must spend in torture, unreprieved.

To which Prometheus replies,

> Perchance no thought can count them, yet they pass.

Shelley's meaning, I take it, is that the redemption of Prometheus and of man, man's growth into the spirit of Christ and his rejection of cruelty and hate, though ultimately certain if man's will to endure persists, is vastly remote. The overthrow of the evil gods will be due to no slaves' revolt, no sudden sharp uprising. When the mind and soul of man are enfranchised his outward fetters will fall from him as those of Prometheus at the agency of Hercules.

The furies born of the "all-miscreative brain of Jove" pour up from Hell to "live through" Prometheus "like animal life" and to crawl "like agony" within his "labyrinthine veins." The suggestion of physical torture is horrible, yet it is not this which wrings a groan from Prometheus but the psychic torture born of the visions of man's cruelty—

> . . . the self-contempt implanted
> In young spirits, sense-enchanted—

and the horrors of famine, war, and kingly and priestly tyranny. These are the theme of Voltaire's eloquence. Shelley stamps them with the aphoristic power of verse.

Browning and Francis Thompson have said that Shelley had he lived would have become a Christian. Shelley indeed was, in the definition of some, a Christian and an excellent one. To others he was agnostic, heretic, atheist. The terminology is of no importance. What Shelley thought both of Christ and of Christianity is set forth unmistakably in the passage beginning,

> One came forth of gentle worth,
> Smiling on the sanguine earth;

His words outlived him, like swift poison
Withering up truth, peace, and pity.

Again in the description of the crucified Christ beginning,

Remit the anguish of that lighted stare . . .

Shelley recounts, after Voltaire and others fired with a sacred
hate of bigotry, the horror of religious persecution in blighting
the life of man.

Thy name I will not speak—
It hath become a curse.

Therein Shelley states precisely his opinion of ecclesiasticism.
But in his depiction of Christ there is a vast difference between
the bitter hatred of *Queen Mab* and the sorrowing heartfelt
love and compassion of *Prometheus Unbound*. It may be said
truthfully that *Prometheus Unbound* is written in the spirit
of Christ; that Prometheus, the Titan, is a symbol both of
Christ and of humanity. Humanity in the person of Prometheus is crucified as Christ was crucified and becomes free only
as it achieves the compassion and the love of Christ. Shelley
accepts the ethics of Christ and rejects all else of Christianity.

To most of the radical young men of England in 1793 the
Reign of Terror was the beginning of disillusionment, which
with the dictatorship of Napoleon became complete. Of the
men of letters of this generation only two of any distinction
remained radical through the black years, Leigh Hunt and
Hazlitt. Shelley had never to experience such disillusionment
as theirs. Born later than they, to him the hopes and the failures of the French Revolution were a part of his education.
In his passion for ideas seemingly so discredited by the realities
of political life Shelley reveals his visionary character, his faith
in the power of ideas to rule the world. It is singular that he
could hold faith with doctrines which even their spokesmen
recanted, and too, with the apparent evidence of their failure

before him. Shelley, notwithstanding these failures, had his
youthful fling at preaching reform and learned by bitter experience that the world repudiates all who do it disinterested
service. The failure of the French Revolution, as he came to
know, was the inevitable expression of man's inability in the
large to live up to the best ideals of a few.

Nevertheless in a kind of despair Shelley, in three suc-
cessive works, *Queen Mab, The Revolt of Islam,* and *Prometheus Unbound,* preaches revolution and describes the better
world to be. Faith in that world he holds to the last. To
renounce it would be wholly to despair. But the day of its
realization becomes in his faith more and more remote until
in *Prometheus Unbound* it is at the end of a time so far that

> the reluctant mind
> Flags wearily in its unending flight.

Shelley is no social visionary in *Prometheus Unbound*. The
golden age is to come as the reward not of revolution but of
the slow ethical change in man himself. Man must become a
kind of god before he is free.

In his description of life as it now is, in the reign of Jupiter,
Shelley is an impassioned and unblinking realist. It has been
said that Shelley shrieks. The criticism is true only of his
more youthful verse. In *Prometheus Unbound* and the other
work of his last period he burns, if not with a "hard gem-like
flame," with the flame, rather, of a volcano. There is fire in
his verse, devastating fire. If mankind had the integrity and
courage to face reality, if words meant anything to it, the
description of the cruelty and horror of life, of man-made life,
as Shelley paints it, would be intolerable:

> In each human heart terror survives
> The ravin it has gorged: the loftiest fear
> All that they would disdain to think were true.

Hypocrisy and custom make their minds
The fanes of many a worship, now outworn.
They dare not devise good for man's estate,
And yet they know not that they do not dare.
The good want power, but to weep barren tears.
The powerful goodness want: worse need for them.
The wise want love; and those who love want wisdom;
And all best things are thus confused to ill.

These are the words of the Fury spoken to torture Prometheus. Were they not true they could not effect their purpose. They are intolerable if man is to be without hope of a better future. Swift had some such terrible vision of life, such inhuman sanity, and it drove him mad. Shelley in his last great years, driven from an active life, a life of practical social service, to a contemplative introspective life, attains the same intolerable sanity of outlook. The despairing hope of a better world, of some far off divine event, kept him throughout his life-time from madness. But at the end he was, I believe, on the verge of it or of suicide, if indeed his drowning was not in itself virtually suicide, a deliberate tempting of fate which is in effect the same. The visionary hope of a better earth-world he clings to until the last, but it is a despairing hope:

The world is weary of the past,
Oh, might it die or rest at last!

An other-worldly religious faith, pursuit of the opiates of pleasure, a profound sense of humor—in any one of these a man may escape the intolerable face of actuality. Shelley was too little fleshly to pursue pleasure, and his sense of humor was slight, certainly not sufficient for him to look upon humanity lightly and find pleasure in its stupidities. It was only in some form of other-worldliness that there was, for him, escape. The traditional faiths, the established churches, were, for many reasons, impossible to him. It was in neo-Platonic mysticism

that he found the faith which he clung to increasingly, as his
poems bear witness, during the last four years of his life.
Whether this mysticism marks in him the growth of faith,
conviction, belief, or rather his efforts to escape despair, it is
not easy to say. Despair and hope alternate, but beneath both
is impatience with the burden of earthly existence. Shelley in
his thirty years had, as he said, lived a hundred. If earthly life
was all, it was intolerable. If it was the shadow only of real
existence, the sooner he had done with phantoms the better.
From *Prometheus Unbound* to the last, in the four years of
his best work, these moods are dominant.

> The grave hides all things beautiful and good.

To the Titan despairing of humanity as he contemplates
the failure of the French Revolution the Earth speaks in con-
solation:

> I bid ascend those subtle and fair spirits,
> Whose homes are the dim caves of human thought,
> And who inhabit, as birds wing the wind,
> Its world-surrounding ether; they behold
> Beyond that twilight realm, as in a glass,
> The future.

The idea here expressed is neo-Platonic and introduces one of
Shelley's most common symbols, the cave, whose probable
origin, as Mr. W. B. Yeats has pointed out, is in Porphyry,
and in the commentary of Thomas Taylor upon neo-Platonic
ideas and symbols in which he discusses Porphyry's concepts.

This oft-repeated image recurs in other passages and with
related symbols which ask interpretation. Taylor remarks of
its origin: "From hence as it appears to me the Pythagorians,
and after them Plato, took occasion to call the world a cave
and a den." The allusion to Plato is, no doubt, to the well-
known passage in which human life is likened to a cave in

which the images of actuality are but the shadows cast upon its wall from reality without. The likeness here is of human existence, the phenomenal world, to a cave; but Shelley is fond of employing the image to symbolize also the individual mind, especially in its in-dwelling, its introspective phase. A few instances from other of his poems will suffice to establish his usage:

> Then from the caverns of my dreamy youth
> I sprang, as one sandalled with plumes of fires
> —*Epipsychidion*, ll. 217-18.

> But a friend's bosom
> Is as the inmost cave of our own mind.
> —*The Cenci*, II, 2, 89.

> . . . and could by patience find
> An entrance to the caverns of his mind.
> —*Julian and Maddalo*, ll. 572-73.

The "subtle and fair spirits whose homes are the dim caves of human thought" but "who inhabit . . . its world-surrounding ether" are not so easily explicable as the cave. They behold, beyond the twilight realm of earth, the future. This fact betrays philosophically their neo-Platonic origin and it is in the light of general neo-Platonic ideas that I would explain Shelley's meaning, harmonizing it with passages of a similar character elsewhere to be found in *Prometheus Unbound*.

It is an idea common to neo-Platonic philosophy in its various expressions that the world of actuality, the phenomenal world existing in time, is a projection or materialization of the ideal world existing in the mind of divinity. This three-fold divinity in two of its hypostases thinks and creates. It is timeless, for the Deity in his contemplative acts perceives each step of the process which, in the material world, unfolds itself in time. To the Deity, past, present, and future are one—the eternal now.

Man in his nature is both of the material world, the world of change operating in time, which he apprehends through reason; and also a part of the divine world, sharing in the mind of God, which is reality. This participation is manifest in his intuitions, his unreasoning perception of divine things— truth, love, beauty. Neo-Platonism insists that the truest knowledge of reality is apprehended intuitively. The reason is a lesser faculty, which, though it may arrive at truth, must do so only after laborious effort. The truths of intuition, revealing as they do the divine nature, are timeless, for they recall perfections which are not in time but in eternity. They are, therefore, to man, who in his lower nature exists in time, prophetic, for they are not yet realized in the lower world of material being. They afford him stay and comfort, assurance that they are prophecies of good to be. This, I take it, is the symbolism of the fair spirits whose home is in man and which yet "inhabit the world-surrounding ether." It is the "phantasy" or imagination which is the intermediary between man's earthly reason and his intuitive perception of divine truth, of truth not yet realized in earthly things. The following comment of Thomas Taylor upon Porphyry is pertinent:

And here it may not be improper to observe, that the phantasy in this purified state, affords indubitable tokens of the possession of truth; and serves as an instrument by which we may discover false opinions from such as are true. For the images attending the perceptions of reality, will always be lucid; and this in proportion to the certainty they contain. Hence, whenever the soul is full, and as it were, pregnant with true conceptions, certain bright phantasms, as the progeny of her rational energies, will drop into the mirror of imagination, and appear like images clothed with light. For the phantasy will now no longer be similar to the dark and irriguous cavern of Calypso (which appears to be the emblem of imagination in an unpurified state), illuminated by sense as by an artificial fire; but it will be totally diaphanous and full of light.

It will, indeed, in every respect resemble the palace of Ithaca, when enlightened by the golden lamp of Minerva. . . .[11]

Another and lesser neo-Platonist, Synesius, also stresses the part played by the imagination in showing the way of the spirit to its true home in the realm of intellectual being. "Imagination is the sense of senses, the one necessary to all the others."[12] And again: "It is great good-fortune to have an intuition of God, but to know God through the instrumentality of the imagination is intuition par excellence."[13] Synesius goes on to say that all things which have existed, do exist, or shall exist cast their images constantly, for matter is forever in a state of flux, and that these images are apprehended by the imagination which reflects them as in a mirror.[14] The images of things yet to be are, however, relatively vague and indistinct as compared to those of the past and present.[15] Both the prophetic character of the visions which come to Prometheus and their real existence as resident in the realm of true being are seemingly declared in the words uttered by these "Spirits":

> From unremembered ages we
> Gentle guides and guardians be
> Of heaven-oppressed mortality.

If these ideas, these dreams of divine love, have forever existed unchanged and have, as man has apprehended them, brought him faith and solace, they are trustworthy auguries of the future. They are a part of the eternal unchanging intellectual world. These comforters of mortality

> . . . breathe, and sicken not
> The atmosphere of human thought.

---

[11] Taylor, *Proclus*, II, 277.

[12] *Oeuvres de Synesius,* par H. Druon. (Paris, Librairie Hachette et cie., 1878), Des Songes, p. 6.

[13] *Ibid.*   [14] *Ibid.*, p. 20.   [15] *Ibid.*

The world of thought, of intellectual being, is one in which man, too, has a share:

> As the thoughts of man's own mind
> Float through all above the grave;
> We make there our liquid lair,
> Voyaging cloudlike and unpent
> Through the boundless element:
> Thence we bear the prophecy
> Which begins and ends in thee!

The metaphor is a variant upon that of the sea as the symbol of the unity of all being. The universality of thought is like the atmosphere which, too, is a sea

> Silent, liquid, and serene.

This aërial sea of thought is the divine intelligence, but man's thoughts as they

> Float through all above the grave

have also their home in it. This is good Platonism. It is in his higher intelligence, not his earthly and mortal nature, that man shares the divine.

The visions divinely borne from the realm of true intellectual being and prophetic of the future depict the triumph of love over tyranny and "creeds outworn." Man's divinity is prophesied in the incident

> Of one who gave an enemy
> His plank, then plunged aside to die.

The Third Spirit tells of a "Dream with plumes of flame" which comforted a Sage and which, being the same as that

> Which had kindled long ago
> Pity, eloquence, and woe,

must therefore be prophetic of its realization. The Fourth Spirit, similarly, tells of the thoughts and dreams of a poet:

> Nor seeks nor finds he mortal blisses,
> But feeds on the aërial kisses
> Of shapes that haunt thought's wildernesses.

The poet

> . . . will watch from dawn to gloom
> The lake-reflected sun illume
> The yellow bees i' the ivy-bloom,
> Nor heed nor see, what things they be;
> But from these create he can
> Forms more real than living man,
> Nurslings of immortality!

The passage has great interest both in its Platonic implication that thought is the sole reality and also, aesthetically, that natural objects serve the poet solely as inspirations to his thought. In their materiality he neither heeds nor sees what they are. They are the point of departure for his own imaginings and the imagination, as has been shown, is the intermediary between the world of sense and the divine world of intellectual being.

In the passage quoted, the lines descriptive of the "lake-reflected sun" and "the yellow bees i' the ivy bloom" are clearly echoes of Plato. In the speech of Ione which immediately follows there are two lines which derive from Dante. The two "shapes from the east and west"

> Come, as two doves to one belovèd nest,
> Twin nurslings of the all-sustaining air.

The coincidence is notable, for evident as is the influence of Plato and of Dante upon Shelley's thought, it is rarely that any passage in Shelley finds in either of them an identifiable verbal parallel. Indeed the influence of many writers is discernible in Shelley's thought, but it is seldom that he borrows words or figures from anyone. *Prometheus Unbound,* though its philosophy is woven of a dozen different strands, is in both thought and form one of the most original of poems.

With the words of the Fifth Spirit who describes the apparition of Love borne

> . . . on lightning-braided pinions,
> Scattering the liquid joy of life. . . .

is introduced a symbolism which in one of its aspects is scientific, the identification of electricity, energy, and light with love. I need not here argue the case for this identification as I have elsewhere done so fully.[16] Further instances I shall note in the progress of the poem and later will consider the implications of Shelley's synthesis.

In the words of the Sixth Spirit and of the chorus which follows, one of Shelley's characteristic uses of the word "shadow" is observable:

Dream visions of aërial joy, and call the monster, Love,
And wake, and find the shadow Pain, as he whom now we greet.

Again:

> Though Ruin now Love's shadow be. . . .

In these instances "shadow" evidently implies that which accompanies something else; is its inevitable, and dark, consequence. I do not see in them any clear neo-Platonic significance, though such a meaning could be extorted. Pain and Ruin may, that is, be thought of as worldly unrealities, misconceptions of the Love whose real existence is not on earth. Such antitheses between the heavenly "real" and the earthly and unreal "shadow" are common enough in Shelley and other instances will be noted. His fondness for the word, and his habitual use of it in several somewhat different though allied meanings, is evidence of his preoccupation with the philosoph-

---

[16] *A Newton Among Poets,* p. 132.

ical problem of reality, true being, versus materiality or seeming. To that problem neo-Platonism supplied the answer which, in his last years, best satisfied him.

The shadow, Ruin, which on "Death's white and wingèd steed" pursues Love and tramples all living things, is to be quelled by Prometheus. So the Spirits predict, and when Prometheus demands,

> Spirits! how know ye this shall be?

the answer is, that as the buds know in the soft winds an assurance of spring, so the Spirits know in the persistence of Wisdom, Justice, Love, and Peace that the effort will be justified in the liberation of Prometheus who is the goal of their prophecy. The assurance is born of intuition. That these forces still live and grow despite the history of their worldly defeat is promise of their ultimate victory. Faith, then, the conviction within the heart, not the evidence of the senses and the judgment of the brain, is reality. This is all in accord with the teachings of Platonism and neo-Platonism. Truth is apprehended by the imagination, which seizes intuitively upon reality. The reason achieves laboriously, if at all, the truth which intuition knows in a flash. Prometheus is somewhat comforted—

> . . . and yet I feel
> Most vain all hope but love, and thou art far,
> Asia!

The words, and Panthea's which follow, introduce one of the knotty points of the poem's philosophical symbolism, the meaning of Asia and of her relationship to Prometheus. An understanding of Shelley's intention here is necessary to the solution of difficulties yet to come.

Mrs. Shelley's words may be taken as a starting point in the interpretation of Asia.

Asia, one of the Oceanides, is the wife of Prometheus—she was, according to other mythological interpretations, the same as Venus and Nature. When the Benefactor of Mankind is liberated, Nature resumes the beauty of her prime, and is united to her husband, the emblem of the human race, in perfect and happy union.

Presumably Mrs. Shelley had this interpretation from the lips of the poet himself. Nor is there any reason to doubt it. Though to it may be added, in the progress of the poem, other meanings derivable from the lines themselves, there is nothing to confuse this, the basic meaning of the symbol.

To a later time and in connection with another passage may be left a more difficult question, the cause of the separation of Asia and Prometheus. Therein is implicit the problem of the origin of evil, and to the elucidation of Shelley's meaning it will be necessary to bring in evidence more of his philosophy than has yet been employed. Evil, for whatever cause, has entered the world, and that evil is symbolized in the separation of the mind of man from nature, with consequences disastrous to both. Man suffers all manner of ill and Nature likewise loses "the beauty of her prime." Panthea describes the scene of Asia's "sad exile," a "far Indian vale" . . .

> . . . rugged once
> And desolate and frozen, like this ravine;
> But now invested with fair flowers and herbs,
> And haunted by sweet airs and sounds, which flow
> Among the woods and waters, from the ether
> Of her transforming presence, which would fade
> If it were mingled not with thine. . . .

The transformation of frozen nature, it is clear, symbolizes the imminent reunion of Asia and Prometheus and his triumph over Jupiter.

Superficially Shelley's meaning in this symbolism is intelligible enough. The difficulty lies in the implication, the philosophy which goes to the root of his system. For he implies, does he not, a unity of man and nature as once existing and as destined again to be? This unity is necessary to the well-being of both; not only does mankind suffer in the separation but nature likewise. Asia, spirit of love and beauty in nature, "a transforming presence," would, in Panthea's words, "fade" were she not mingled with Prometheus. She is depicted, indeed, as more dependent upon him than he upon her. Prometheus endures all loss, all negations of good, strong in his self-sufficiency; but Asia lives only in him. The implication, I take it, is that mind, the mind of man, is the directing force of the universe, and all else subservient to it. The conflict of Prometheus is within the mind itself, a conflict which has its consequences in the physical world, to be sure, but which determines these. True to his neo-Platonic philosophy, then, Shelley seems to say that mind is the only reality, though as the poem develops his theme the term "mind" is rather an inclusive one, meaning not only ratiocination but also imagination and passion. The words of Humphry Davy while under the influence of laughing gas perhaps define Shelley's conception: "Nothing exists but thoughts! the universe is composed of impressions, ideas, pleasures, and pains."[17] Or to cite Shelley's own phrasing of the same belief in *Hellas:*

> Thought
> Alone, and its quick elements, Will, Passion,
> Reason, Imagination, cannot die;
> They are . . . .
> The stuff whence mutability can weave
> All that it hath dominion o'er—
>
> —ll. 795-800.

Whether this interpretation of Shelley's idea is just will more definitely appear in the discussion of the later acts. To the

[17] John Davy, *Memoirs of the Life of Sir Humphry Davy,* 2 vols. (London, Longman, 1836), I, 99.

difficulties of the second act the lines of Panthea near the end
of the first will serve as a convenient bridge; for a determina-
tion of Panthea's place in the poem's symbolism is necessary
to its complete interpretation. Panthea's words are:

> Hast thou forgotten one who watches thee
> The cold dark night, and never sleeps but when
> The shadow of thy spirit falls on her?

What does Panthea symbolize?   And what, too, Ione, sisters both of Asia, the spirit of love and beauty in nature, the
earthly Venus?

SCENE I

THAT THE three Oceanides, Asia, Panthea, and Ione, are sisters gives the key to their symbolic meaning: they are, that is, three aspects of love. From her evident function in the drama, as from Mrs. Shelley's definition, we know Asia to be passionate creative love. The other two, lacking a gloss, must be interpreted by the parts which they play, the words they speak. Inevitably the attempt to catch up in an exact phrase a poetic symbol whose value lies in its suggestion, its varied connotations, is destined to partial failure. It seems necessary nevertheless to make the attempt, for these symbols have beneath their poetic dress an intellectual signification which constitutes their core or kernel. To extract it is to lay violent hands, for the moment, upon the poetic mode of expression. Yet I think the outrage to beauty is but momentary and the method is in the end justified by the very enhancement which it achieves of beauty itself.[1]

Panthea, in Asia's words, is

> The shadow of that soul by which I live,

the shadow, that is, of Prometheus. Yet Prometheus had addressed Panthea in these words:

> Sister of her whose footsteps pave the world
> With loveliness—more fair that aught but her
> Whose shadow thou art—

[1] "Of the sisters Ione and Panthea in Shelley's *Prometheus Unbound*, Ione is the seeing one, Panthea the knowing one. Ione sees first and from a distance, and speaks first; Panthea replies, she discerns and explains. They may be regarded therefore as representing these—two faculties or modes of thought of the mind in general—one seeing, the other analyzing. . . . On the other hand they are sisters of Asia, forming with her one of the familiar trinities, and may thus be regarded as emanations from the mind of Asia and so externally derived. Prometheus is clearly an autogenous character in many features." Frederick Clarke Prescott: *The Poetic Mind* (New York, 1926), p. 207, note.

Panthea then is "shadow" both of the soul of Prometheus and sister and "shadow" of Asia. Most like to, and intimate with, both, she is the bond between them in their long enforced separation. She is the watcher and consoler of Prometheus, and in this first scene of the second act she serves as messenger from him to Asia. The nature and mode of her communication enable us to define her abstract symbolism more precisely.

The communication of which Panthea is the bearer is breathed into her by Prometheus. She is absorbed in him:

> . . . an atmosphere
> Which wrapped me in its all-dissolving power,
> As the warm ether of the morning sun
> Wraps ere it drinks some cloud of wandering dew.
> I saw not, heard not, moved not, only felt
> His presence flow and mingle through my blood
> Till it became his life, and his grew mine,
> And I was thus absorbed, until it passed . . .

Just what it is that Prometheus communicates Panthea does not herself know. Asia reads it in her eyes as though summoning her from the hypnotic trance into which Prometheus had plunged her. It is a justifiable surmise, I believe, that in his dramatization of this conception Shelley employed the technic of mesmerism, of which he had some knowledge.[2]

[2] "We observe," says Mesmer, "the flowing of a certain subtle matter, which penetrates all bodies, without perceptibly losing any of its activity; and this matter operates at considerable distances, without the aid of any intermediate object." Again: "It is by this operation (the most universal which nature exhibits to us) that the relations of activity are maintained between the heavenly bodies, the earth, and its constituent parts. The properties of matter, and of organized bodies, depend upon this operative and modifying principle. The animal body experiences the alternating effects of this universal agent; which, by insinuating itself into the substance of the nerves, affects them immediately. The human body exhibits properties analogous to those of a magnet." J. C. Colquhoun, *An History of Magic, Witchcraft, and Magnetism,* 2 vols. (London, Longman, Brown, Green, & Longmans, 1851), II, 161.

Mesmeric or no in its device, the dream or trance which Asia reads in Panthea's eyes she feels to be an augury of hope:

> Say not those smiles that we shall meet again
> Within that bright pavilion which their beams
> Shall build o'er the waste world?

The dream is succeeded by another which Panthea consciously recalls, a dream of symbolic import. She had dreamt that "yon lightning-blasted almond tree" burst into bud and that a chill wind nipping the blossoms cast them to earth:

> But on each leaf was stamped, as the blue bells
> Of Hyacinth tell Apollo's written grief,
> *Oh, follow, follow!*

Lightning is the symbol of evil power, of love perverted by Jupiter to purposes of destruction. The "lightning-blasted" tree which bursts into blossom is, I take it, an augury that the object of his wrath will flower into a new and beautiful life.

But before pursuing the implications of the symbol and the journey of Asia and Panthea, what further may be said of Panthea's function? What abstraction does she personify? Were not the word "sympathy" too edifying and too little colored with passion I should say that it defined Panthea's rôle. Perhaps the term "sympathetic love" as distinguished from creative love such as is personified in Asia will serve the purpose. Hers is the love which comforts Prometheus and Asia in separation, the love which enables them to know each other's hearts though distant, a love through which each is a likeness of the other. In a sequential reading of *Prometheus Unbound* let us see whether such an interpretation does not fairly define Panthea in her various appearances.

If Panthea is provisionally defined as the symbol of sympathetic love, what then may be said of Ione, whose part in the dramatic machinery of the play is slight and whose character

is to be defined rather by the quality of her perceptions than
by any distinctive action? In the preceding act Ione is depicted
as a character less strong than Panthea, less able to endure
sights of suffering and woe. As the Phantasm of Jupiter is
summoned to appear Ione is made to say,

> My wings are folded o'er mine ears;
> My wings are crossèd o'er mine eyes.

And when the Phantasm is torn "as fire tears a thunder-cloud,"
Ione cries:

> He speaks! Oh shelter me!

Yet Ione is first to comfort Earth and the Echoes who falsely
perceive in Prometheus' repentance of his curse the surrender
of the Titan. And she is first to perceive the coming of beauty
in the form of Mercury:

> Fear not: 'tis but some passing spasm;
> The Titan is unvanquished still.
> But see, where through the azure chasm
>   Of yon forked and snowy hill,
> Trampling the slant winds on high
> With golden-sandalled feet, that glow
> Under plumes of purple dye,
> Like rose-ensanguined ivory,
>   A Shape comes now,
> Stretching on high from his right hand
> A serpent-cinctured wand.

It is Ione, too, who asks who are these "with hydra tresses"?
Panthea says they are "Jove's tempest-walking hounds." Ione
asks again:

> Are they now led from the thin dead
> On new pangs to be fed?

It may be remarked with some justice that in this scene Ione
serves chiefly as an interlocutor, a dramatic device whereby

the necessary description is introduced. Yet her characterization, though slight, is consistent. She is quick to perceive
beauty and shrinks from the sight of evil. When Ione describes the two shapes which

> Come, as two doves to one belovèd nest,

Panthea asks,

> Canst thou speak, sister? all my words are drowned.

And Ione replies:

> Their beauty gives me voice.

Panthea speaking to Asia in scene 1 of Act II thus describes
her slumber before the fall of Prometheus and Asia's unhappy
love:

> . . . erewhile I slept
> Under the glaucous caverns of old Ocean
> Within dim bowers of green and purple moss,
> Our young Ione's soft and milky arms
> Locked then as now behind my dark, moist hair,
> While my shut eyes and cheek were pressed within
> The folded depth of her life-breathing bosom:
> But not as now, since I am made the wind
> Which fails beneath the music that I bear
> Of thy most wordless converse. . . .

In the golden days before the coming of Jupiter, Panthea

> . . . was wont to sleep
> Peacefully, and awake refreshed and calm

—lines which in their context recall other lines:

> Then radiant, as the mind arising bright
> From the embrace of beauty . . .

It is not, to be sure, certain that in these two passages Shelley's
idea is the same; but he is fond of repeating his images, and
the identification of Ione with beauty of perception, or, to

make her sisterhood with Panthea and Asia more evident, the
Spirit of Love in Beauty, pretty well meets the requirements
of our interpretation.[3] It will be useful, at any rate, thus provisionally to define her and seek in the later passages of the
poem to approve or reject this reading.

The symbolism inherent in Panthea and Ione has, then,
tentatively, emerged from this discussion of Panthea's dramatic service as messenger. The dream which Asia reads in
her eyes revives the memory of Asia's dream of similar import.
Alike, on the fallen almond blossoms and "on the shadows of
the moving clouds" is written "Follow, Oh, Follow"—what
and where the drama is to unfold. There is in these passages
much beautiful descriptive poetry upon which it is not my
intention to comment, my concern being with the dramatic
devices, symbolism, and latent philosophic meaning. Yet I
cannot but observe that Shelley's symbolism in Panthea, the
mesmeric character of her trance, and Asia's reading of the
dream are to my taste unduly tenuous and difficult. Dramatically the upshot of it all is that Prometheus conveys thereby
to Asia the command to "Follow," an idea which Asia recalls
also from her own dream. This command is presumably an
intuition of the impending change in the fortunes of the chief
character. I find it in me to wish that Shelley had employed
a simpler and more intelligible apparatus to effect his end.

The echoes repeat the mysterious command, but these are
not echoes, rather spirit voices which summon Asia and Panthea to pursue them "through the caverns hollow," the "noontide darkness," the "woodland noontide dew," "the fountain-
lighted caves." Again, we encounter the caves, symbol of
human existence shut in from reality, or of the inward-looking

[3] I am indebted in this interpretation of the function of Ione and in other
unacknowledged instances to an unpublished paper by Anna Gates Butler,
which better than any other interpretation I have read makes some phases of
the allegory within the poem consistent and intelligible.

mind whose meditations are lighted by fountains. What are these fountains? Taylor citing from the *Hymn to Apollo* in his commentary on Proclus makes their meaning clear:

The nymphs residing in caves shall deduce fountains of intellectual waters to thee, (according to the divine voice of the Muses,) which are the progeny of a terrene spirit.

The scene which follows, depicting the journey of Asia and Panthea, leads us even deeper into neo-Platonic symbolism.

SCENE II

This scene is one of the most difficult in the poem, but its interpretation perhaps better than any other reveals the mixed scientific and neo-Platonic character of Shelley's symbolism. It is purely lyric, comprised of choruses of spirits speaking antiphonally, and of the speeches of the two fauns. It is these last which open the way to an interpretation which would otherwise easily escape the reader seduced by the lyric beauty of the lines. For the speeches of the fauns may be definitely and exactly interpreted. The spirits of which the fauns speak, those "which make such delicate music in the woods," are the elements of which matter is composed. I have elsewhere[4] demonstrated that the bubbles which the sun sucks from the water-flowers are hydrogen gas, for the passage descriptive of the process closely resembles a passage in Erasmus Darwin to which Darwin's notes give this specific meaning.[5] Likewise those others which "live under pink blossoms" or "within the bells of meadow flowers" are other elements which the chemistry of nature creates for the uses of vegetation. It is an extraordinary instance of Shelley's use of science for poetic purposes; and it points the way to the elucidation of the scene as a whole.

[4] *A Newton Among Poets*, p. 172.
[5] *Ibid.*, p. 173.

It is to the cave of Demogorgon, mysterious source of all things, the sphynx whom they seek to question as to the meaning of God, life, and evil, that Asia and Panthea make their way through the "forest intermingled with rocks and caverns." They are seeking reality, the inner meaning of visible forms. In the world of matter the answer is implicit in the dialogue of the fauns, for the spirits of which these speak are the personified chemical elements which in their various combinations constitute inanimate matter and which in their cyclical round, as instanced in the hydrogen atom, are a part of the life history of plant and animal. What, then, is the symbolism of the forest, the flowers and nightingales, the growth so dense that only an occasional cloud of dew or beam of starlight can penetrate it? The answer to this is to be found not in scientific but in neo-Platonic sources.

In a notable passage Thomas Taylor in his *Proclus* interprets the symbolism of Calypso and her cave, an interpretation which, however fanciful as a reading of Homer, is invaluable as a clue to Shelley's employment of symbols in *Prometheus Unbound*. Several symbols which Taylor defines Shelley uses in the same or similar ways.

That the poet then by Calypso occultly signifies the phantasy, is I think evident from his description of her abode, (for the anonymous Greek author, affords us no farther assistance). For she is represented as dwelling in a cavern, illuminated by a great fire; and this cave, is surrounded with a thick wood, is watered by four fountains, and is situated in an island, far remote from any habitable parts, and invironed by the mighty ocean. All which particulars correspond with the phantasy, as I presume the following observations will evince. In the first place then, as the phantasy is situated between sense and cogitation, it communicates with each in such a manner that its beginning is the end of the cogitative power, and its end is the commencement of the senses. Hence on account of its two-fold nature it partakes of a twofold light; receiving in its supreme part the splendor of cogitation, and in its inferior part, a light corresponding to that of sense. Now it is this inferior part or the common phantasy, which is represented by the cave of Calypso, for its light is artificial and external like that of fire: and this correspondence is evident from the etymology of the phantasy, which is derived from . . . *light.* In the next place the island is said to be surrounded with a thick wood, which evidently corresponds to a material nature, or this humid body, with which the phantasy is invested: for . . . *a wood* implies matter according to its primary signification. But the four fountains by which the cave is watered occultly intimate those four gnostic powers of the soul discovered by the Pythagoreans, and embraced by Plato: *intelligence, cogitation, opinion,* and *imagination.* And these fountains are said, with great propriety and correspondence to communicate with each other. In the last place the island is said to be invironed with the ocean, which admirably agrees with a corporeal nature, forever flowing without admitting any periods of repose. And thus much for the secret agreement of the cavern and island with the regions of imagination.[6]

Again, according to Plato, the deep, the sea, and a tempest are so many symbols of the constitution of matter: and on this account, I think, the poet called that part by the name of the marine god Phorcys.[7]

"Wood" and "wilderness," then, in the passage in *Prometheus Unbound* symbolize the realm of earthly existence which is shut away from the reality of heaven. It implies, I think, the external world of things, the corporeal body, and also the mind itself. Asia's journey thus symbolizes a return to the source of things, to reality, in a twofold sense. She passes to the atomic basis of matter and she also penetrates beyond the deceptions of bodily sensations to the reality of intellectual knowledge. The choruses of spirits chant the intoxications of the senses in this "forest" shut out from the life of heaven. Eye and ear are drugged with beauty:

> There the voluptuous nightingales,
>   Are awake through all the broad noon-day.

[6] Taylor, *Proclus,* II, 300-1, note.   [7] *Ibid.,* pp. 294-95.

When one with bliss or sadness fails,
  And through the windless ivy-boughs,
   Sick with sweet love, droops dying away
On its mate's music-panting bosom;
Another from the swinging blossom,
   Watching to catch the languid close
  Of the last strain, then lifts on high
  The wings of the weak melody,
Till some new stream of feeling bear
  The song, and all the woods are mute;
When there is heard through the dim air
The rush of wings, and rising there,
  Like many a lake-surrounded flute,
Sounds overflow the listener's brain
So sweet, that joy is almost pain.

These are the pleasures of sense; but earthly life of which
these are the allurements

   Is curtained out from Heaven's wide blue;
  Nor sun, nor moon, nor wind, nor rain,
    Can pierce its interwoven bowers,
    Nor aught, save when some cloud of dew,
Drifted along the earth-creeping breeze
Between the trunks of the hoar trees,
   Hangs each a pearl in the pale flowers
  Of the green laurel, blown anew;
And bends, and then fades silently,
One frail and fair anemone:
Or when some star of many a one
That climbs and wanders through steep night,
Has found the cleft through which alone
Beams fall from high those depths upon,
Ere it is borne away, away,
By the swift Heavens that cannot stay,
It scatters drops of golden light,
Like lines of rain that ne'er unite.

The symbolism of dew as a token of divine love, of a heavenly
influence which penetrates even through the thick forest of

man's sensual enslavement, will be evident from the employment of the symbol in this meaning elsewhere in Shelley's
verse.   Dew is a word used many times by Shelley, often in a
literal sense but often, too, with the implication of balm, love,
and heavenly thought.   The meaning of it in the passage
under consideration is made clear by lines in *Hellas* wherein
the symbolic implication of the term is explicitly defined.

> Within the circuit of this pendant orb
> There lies an antique region, on which fell
> The dews of thought in the world's golden dawn
> Earliest and most benign, and from it sprung
> Temples and cities and immortal forms
> And harmonies of wisdom and of song,
> And thoughts, and deeds worthy of thoughts so fair.
> And when the sun of its dominion failed,
> And when the winter of its glory came,
> The winds that stripped it bare blew on, and swept
> That dew into the utmost wildernesses
> In wandering clouds of sunny rain that thawed
> The unmaterial bosom of the North.
>   —Prologue, ll. 31-43.

The meaning of this passage is unmistakable. The intellectual
inspiration of Greek culture was disseminated, after the fall of
the Greek civilization, in the "wildernesses" of the northern
countries. Dews, then, are divinely inspired thoughts and the
wilderness is a symbol of the unenlightened mind. Thus,
similarly, Asia's journey is through the labyrinth or wilderness
of the mind, which, though seduced by the senses, has yet its
moments of divine knowledge and inspiration as symbolized
by the "dews of thought."

The star, likewise, whose beams fleetingly pierce the woodland roof, is symbolical of things spiritual. Of the many ex-
amples which might be adduced from Shelley's verse of the
heavenly associations of the term these two instances may

suffice, significant too in that they are from *The Revolt of Islam* in which the symbolism employed is often the same as that of *Prometheus Unbound* but more obviously and intelligibly employed:

> O Love, who to the hearts of wandering men
> Art as the calm to Ocean's weary waves!
> . . . .
> Guide us as one clear star the seaman saves.
> —*The Revolt of Islam,* VIII, xi, 1-2, 5.

And again:

> Fair star of life and love. . . .
> —*The Revolt of Islam,* IX, xxxvi, 5.

In *The Revolt of Islam,* too, it is the Morning Star which, falling in combat with the blood-red comet, remains on earth in likeness of the serpent as the principle of good eternally at war with evil. The star-beams which penetrate the woodland which Asia traverses are to be thought of then as the light from heaven, as flashes from the intellectual being, intuitive knowledge of the divine, or tokens of divine love.

The "wilderness" may be thought of broadly as the world of sense, of all corporeal phenomena. But there is evidence also that Shelley employs the term sometimes to mean the mind itself. Mrs. Shelley, in her notes on *Prometheus Unbound,* says that she had found in one of Shelley's manuscript books "remarks on a line in the Oedipus Tyrannus," a line which he translates as

'Coming to many ways in the wanderings of careful thought.'

Of this Shelley remarks, "What a picture does this line suggest of the mind as a wilderness of intricate paths, wide as the universe, which is here made its symbol; a world within a world which he, who seeks some knowledge with respect to what he ought to do searches throughout, as he would search

the external universe for some valued thing which was hidden
from him upon its surface." The wilderness, then, is either
the internal universe of the mind or the external world of
sensible things. The reality which Asia seeks lies back of
both, but is in the life of the mind manifest in occasional
flashes or intuitions—the dew and the star-beams of Shelley's
figure.

The song of the semi-chorus which preludes the speech of
the fauns, the meaning of whose dialogue in scientific terms
we have seen, is one of the most important in the poem insofar as it throws light on Shelley's philosophy and symbolism.
It is a key passage, that in which the dual symbolism he employs is reconciled.

Semi-chorus I

> There those enchanted eddies play
> Of echoes, music-tongued, which draw,
> By Demogorgon's mighty law,
> With melting rapture, or sweet awe,
> All spirits on that secret way,
> As inland boats are driven to Ocean
> Down streams made strong with mountain-thaw;
> And first there comes a gentle sound
> To those in talk or slumber bound,
> And wakes the destined; soft emotion
> Attracts, impels them; those who saw
> Say from the breathing earth behind
> There steams a plume-uplifting wind
> Which drives them on their path, while they
> Believe their own swift wings and feet
> The sweet desires within obey;
> And so they float upon their way,
> Until, still sweet, but loud and strong,
> The storm of sound is driven along,
> Sucked up and hurrying; as they fleet,
> Behind, its gathering billows meet

And to the fatal mountain bear
Like clouds amid the yielding air.

The parallelisms of this passage to that which succeeds, the speech of the fauns descriptive of the mutations of hydrogen, are close. The hydrogen, through the action of the sun upon the water plants, escapes into the atmosphere where the atoms "flow like meteors through the night" and where, uniting with oxygen through the operation of electricity, water is formed and the drops

. . . glide in fire
Under the waters of the earth again.

This same round of life is repeated in the lives of spirits seduced into earthly incarnation by the lure of the senses and the emotions:

All spirits on that secret way,
As inland boats are driven to Ocean
Down streams made strong with mountain-thaw.

The figure is one which, in various applications, Shelley frequently employs: the likeness of the individual soul to a boat driven down an inland stream to join the universal sea. This is the round of being which ocean, cloud, rain, and stream aptly symbolize, a symbol of which Shelley is most fond. An excellent and clear instance which employs the figure in most of its aspects is to be found in *The Revolt of Islam:*

We know not where we go, or what sweet dream
May pilot us through caverns strange and fair
Of far and pathless passion, while the stream
Of life our bark doth on its whirlpools bear,
Spreading swift wings as sails to the dim air;
Nor should we seek to know, so the devotion
Of love and gentle thoughts be heard still there
Louder and louder from the utmost Ocean
Of universal life, attuning its commotion.
—VI, xxix.

The mutations of matter as symbolized in the cloud, depicting the cyclical history of the hydrogen atom drawn from the sea to the sky and then home again to its source, are paralleled by the life history of the souls drawn from the ocean of universal being, individually incarnated, and returning again to their source. This figure likening the soul to water is derived from the neo-Platonic concept of the earthly vehicle of the soul as humid. In the passage earlier cited from Thomas Taylor's *Proclus* (see p. 26) it is said that the soul descending to earth "attracts a humid spirit . . . she attracts moisture. But when she endeavors to depart from nature, she becomes a dry splendor, without a shadow, and without a cloud: for humidity constitutes a cloud in the air; but dryness produces from vapour, a dry splendor."

Doubtless the employment of water as the earthly vehicle of the soul is a natural and inevitable metaphor, insomuch as it is the most mobile form of matter which yet retains its intrinsic character throughout its many mutations. Another and kindred analogy, one too which Shelley constantly employs, is that of the boat as symbol of the soul's "vehicle." This, too, is neo-Platonic in origin. Taylor writes:

But the soul in its first descent, derives this spirit from the planetary spheres, and entering this as a boat associates itself with the corporeal world.

The origin, then, of Shelley's most pervasive symbol, that of the cloud as typifying both the mutations of matter and the life history of the soul, is evident. It is to be found both in science and in neo-Platonism. In developing the figure in the double sense Shelley works out its correspondences in a detailed and consistent fashion. The Spirits, obeying the law of Demogorgon, are seduced by the "echoes, music-tongued." The "soft emotion" awakened in them impels them to obey

the "sweet desires within"; then as in a storm, a storm of
cloud-like music, the souls caught up in it are borne to the
fatal mountain

> Like clouds amid the yielding air.

The figure is complex. The storm which impels the souls is
first likened to music—the divine harmony of the eternal law;
the souls compose the clouds of this storm, clouds which are
borne to the "fatal mountain" of earthly incarnation. For as
a cloud borne against a mountain by the wind is precipitated
in rain, so the souls swept by the divine law (harmony) and
yielding to the allurements of sense are incarnated as individuals in earthly life. They are now separate and apart, and
their earthly course is to retrace by spring, brook, and river
their way to the sea of universal being whence they came.
The analogy of the life history of the atom of water to the
life history of the soul is thus complete. The cloud symbolically represents this mutation common to matter and to
spirit.

Another passage from Thomas Taylor reënforces the conclusions already reached:

Besides he [Homer] knew that the gates of heaven were committed to the care of the hours, commencing in cloudy places; and
which are opened and shut by the clouds: for he says,
> Whether they unfold, or close a dense cloud.
Hence likewise they are said to resound because thunders roar
through the clouds.
> Heaven's gates spontaneous open to the powers,
> Heaven's sounding gates kept by the winged hours.[7a]

Why the souls must descend into generation is variously
explained in neo-Platonic philosophy. Sometimes the reason
assigned is necessity; again, some mystic need of experience;
and yet again the "allurements of pleasure":

[7a] *Ibid.*, p. 290.

Hence those who desire to evocate departed souls, sacrifice to them with milk sweetened with honey: convinced that by the allurements of pleasure, these souls would desire to pass into generation.

In the passage from *Prometheus Unbound* under discussion Shelley evidently assigns as the cause of the earthly generation of souls desire which, thinking itself free, is really the working of necessity. I do not wish at the moment to discuss the larger implications of this idea, the problem of free will and necessity. These will be considered elsewhere. It is sufficient for the present to summarize the meaning of this subtle scene with its difficult but precise parallels of scientific and neo-Platonic symbolism: Asia and Panthea are reversing the process of life, moving backward in time through the generation of souls and through the basic elements of matter to that preëxistence which only is reality. Asia's song at the end of the second act defines this Platonic concept explicitly:

> We have passed Age's icy caves,
> And Manhood's dark and tossing waves,
> And Youth's smooth ocean, smiling to betray;
> Beyond the glassy gulfs we flee
> Of shadow-peopled Infancy,
> Through Death and Birth to a diviner day.

SCENE III

The brief third scene is largely descriptive, Asia in a long passage exclaiming upon the beauty of creation:

> How glorious art thou, Earth! and if thou be
> The shadow of some spirit lovelier still,
> Though evil stain its work, and it should be
> Like its creation, weak yet beautiful,
> I could fall down and worship that and thee.

The Platonism is evident. Earth is the shadow of some lovelier spirit, for all things in the world of the actual are but

approximations—shadows—of the divine reality of archetyp-
ical forms. The suggested note of weakness in the creative
spirit whereby evil stains its work implies a God not wholly
omnipotent, one engaged in doubtful strife with the principle
of evil. The implications of this thesis, one vital to an understanding of Shelley's philosophy, are more fully suggested,
however, in those later passages in which Asia puts her questions to Demogorgon.

Of the remainder of the scene, the opening lines and the
concluding song are the parts of greatest philosophic interest.
The "mighty portal" to the realm of Demogorgon is likened to

> . . . . a volcano's meteor-breathing chasm,
> Whence the oracular vapor is hurled up
> Which lonely men drink wandering in their youth,
> And call truth, virtue, love, genius, or joy,
> That maddening wine of life, whose dregs they drain
> To deep intoxication . . .

The scientific implications of the passage I have elsewhere
discussed: the relationship of volcanoes to "falling stones," or
meteors; and the inebriating vapors which, it is supposed,
were the means to the prophetic trance of priest or priestess
at the shrines of oracles.[8] There is in these lines, however, a
second meaning, an implied simile. The oracular vapor which
emanates from the chasm is the "maddening wine of life";
lonely men in youth call it "truth, virtue, love, genius, joy."
It is, seemingly, a source of inspiration, and those who are in-
toxicated by it uplift their voice "which is contagion to the
world."

The meaning of the passage turns upon the significance of
Demogorgon and the cave or realm in which he dwells. If, as
we have seen, Asia and Panthea have journeyed to the home
of that reality which lies behind the illusions of matter and the

[8] *A Newton Among Poets,* pp. 183-188.

deceptions of sense, they come to the mysterious source of creation symbolized by the dark and formless power of Demogorgon. From that source of things, of matter in its various shapes, springs also the creative spirit of man himself, manifested in love, genius, and joy—"the maddening wine of life." That Demogorgon is, in one of his capacities, to be identified with this creative spirit, with that phase of divinity which makes manifest the ideas of the One, is increasingly evident as the thought of the poem unfolds.

To his realm Asia and Panthea are summoned by spirits which seem to personify the fiery and electric essence of matter—

> A countenance with beckoning smiles; there burns
> An azure fire within its golden locks!
> Another and another: hark! they speak!

But it is to a deeper and darker reality that the spirits guide them—

> To the deep, to the deep,
>   Down, down!
> Through the shade of sleep,
> Through the cloudy strife
> Of Death and of Life;
> Through the veil and the bar
> Of things which seem and are . . .

The realm to which they go is that in which

> . . . there is one pervading, one alone. . . .

It is beyond all form and color, all visible and physical manifestations, for it is that occult negation whence matter and force come into being. There

> A spell is treasured but for thee alone.

The first four stanzas of the song and the similes drawn from the realm of matter are intelligible enough in their scientific implications, but the fifth and concluding stanza is somewhat more recondite:

> Resist not the weakness,
> Such strength is in meekness
> That the Eternal, the Immortal
> Must unloose through life's portal
> The snake-like Doom coiled underneath his throne
> By that alone.

Meekness, personified in Prometheus, is in some way to triumph and avert the Doom coiled beneath the throne of the Eternal. I find this a hard saying and my reading of it I submit with diffidence, though I believe it to be in accord with the philosophy of the poem as to this point expounded and as more conclusively set forth in subsequent scenes.

The Doom beneath the throne of the Eternal I take to be the enslavement of the will of man (Prometheus) through submission to his own creation (Jupiter), a submission averted by Prometheus when he repents the curse he had passed upon Jupiter. For the meekness of that repentance is in reality strength: in his moral supremacy Prometheus no longer subserves evil; he asserts the freedom of the moral will. Ethically this is to proclaim the truth of Christ's exhortation to overcome evil by love. Metaphysically the point is somewhat subtler and less easily phrased. Seemingly this Doom—the fatality, I take it, of Necessity—is inherent in the scheme of creation, unless living creatures, the creation of the Eternal, shall attain through their own free choice—through the exercise of the moral will—to a mastery of evil and proclaim the omnipotence of love. To declare thus their acceptance of Love as the ruling force of the universe is for them to be reunited with the One. But the choice must be free not coerced. So Shelley, I take it, implies, with manifold implications which attest that he had brooded long on the Christian mysteries and the symbolism of Christ, the Redeemer.

Scene iv

The Journey to the Cave of Demogorgon symbolizes a return to the source both of material and of spiritual existence. In the material round of creation this return is exemplified in water and its cyclical journey from ocean to cloud and back again to ocean. In the congruent imagery of neo-Platonism, souls likewise are drawn from the ocean of universal mind to the clouds which are borne by the wind of desire. The clouds driven against the "fatal mountain" spill their burden. The souls form rivulets which come again at last to the parent ocean. The source of all is the dim mysterious cave of creation where Demogorgon is enthroned.

The importance of the cave in Shelley's symbolism has already been noted. It is variously employed, but the meanings are intelligible in their similarity. The idea common to all is of something shut away, occult, mysterious. Thus the world is a cave, as in Plato's parable, because shut away from the reality of heaven. Even more is the individual mind a cave in which the soul broods alone, illumined only by intuitions and mysterious questionings which are symbolized by the "intellectual fountains." Shelley speaks of the caves of youth and of "age's icy caves." Some of the varied uses of the symbol will be apparent in *Prometheus Unbound*. The present instance, the cave of Demogorgon, in its obscurity and remoteness evidently implies the mystery of the origin of things. It will be noted that Demogorgon, though manifested in speech and act, is never visible. He remains

. . . . a mighty darkness
Filling the seat of power. . . .

The Miltonic echo in the description is evident but, as I have elsewhere endeavored to show, Shelley endows the traditional image with another meaning borrowed from science. Herschel's dark rays[9] were evidently in his mind no less than the poetical images of Milton and Spenser. Demogorgon in *Prometheus Unbound* is more than one of the lesser potentates of Hades. Shelley conceives him in the meaning of the ancient myth to be father of the gods and coeval with the fates. Demogorgon is the symbol of Necessity, obscure parent of all created things and subservient in Shelley's theology only to Love.

The form of Demogorgon is veiled, but the "mighty darkness" which only is manifest once the veil is drawn, is itself formless, symbolizing the occult nature of the source of things, which is not to be understood even when visible. It is to Demogorgon, an ultimate power, then, that Asia puts her questions and from this mysterious power receives her riddling answers. In them lies much of Shelley's philosophy, which, though difficult, is intelligible and consistent. The crux of the interpretation of it lies in the definition of the ultimate power or powers of the universe and the relation thereto of Demogorgon, Prometheus, and Jupiter.

Demogorgon can tell all that Asia dare demand, and to her questions, who made the living world and all that it contains, gives the one answer, God, Almighty God. It is *Merciful* God, too,

> Who made that sense which, when the winds of spring
> In rarest visitation, or the voice
> Of one belovèd heard in youth alone,
> Fills the faint eyes with falling tears. . . .

The creative and merciful God is clearly also the God of beauty.

But when Asia asks Demogorgon to name the author of

[9] *Ibid.,* p. 154.

all the misery of life, of "terror, madness, crime, remorse," of "self-contempt," of "pain"

> And Hell, or the sharp fear of Hell,

the answer is no longer God but the significant "He reigns." It is evident that God the Creator and God the Merciful does not reign in man's universe. Asia again demands the name of the usurper but Demogorgon repeats only, "He reigns." Thereupon Asia recounts, in a long speech, the history of the material universe, a most interesting mixture of legend, myth, science, history, and metaphysics which asks an extended analysis.

At the first was the Heaven and Earth and Light and Love, an eternal timeless universe in which Saturn ruled,

> . . . from whose throne
> Time fell, an envious shadow. . . .

The thought is familiar to Platonic and neo-Platonic philosophy. God and reality are timeless, but the creation of the material universe, the "realization" of it in matter, necessitates time "the envious shadow." I am not sure that the idea is wholly intelligible, for it is impossible for human thought to move other than in time. Time, in Kant's phrase, is an antinomy. If a timeless universe is conceivable, it is not in the reason it is so, but only as a state of mystical apprehension, whence doubtless the idea has entered philosophy. However this may be, we are not called upon at this point to justify it nor Shelley's employment of it, as he is only following in the steps of the mystical philosophers; to state its origin satisfies our immediate purpose.

The age which Asia depicts in the earlier lines of her speech is the traditional "golden age" of Greek myth, the Garden of Eden of Christian mythology; it is also the state of primitive innocence, the state of nature dear to the French revolutionary school of thought. The coincidence of these beliefs is interesting, but of the three the Christian myth has, I think, least weight with Shelley despite the reason for the fall, which, the thirst for knowledge, is the same in the Christian and the Platonic philosophies.

The question underlying, the problem of evil entering a happy and innocent world, is a profound one and must be debated to determine, if no more, whence Shelley derived it and how, if at all, he alters it to his own philosophic scheme.

In Platonism and neo-Platonism are several theories as to the origin of evil, their number being in itself evidence of philosophic uncertainty on the point. In Proclus it is intimated that the souls enter human life desirous of bodily sensation, a descent into fleshliness, a theory which Shelley himself has expressed in the preceding scene in his symbolism of water and the cloud, though there, it is to be remembered, Necessity is the ultimate cause and the souls, though thinking themselves free, are not in reality so. Plato's speculations also are various and not consistent:

Again it should be noted that, as with Plato, Shelley's God is only doubtfully omnipotent; Plato does not appear to solve to his own satisfaction the problem of evil; faced with the dilemma that either 'He is not good or not omnipotent,' Plato decides for the latter half of the dilemma and limits his Deity's omnipotence. In his later works, at least, he speaks as if there were a powerful spirit of evil interfering with the Supreme and marring its work. In the *Timaeus* the God of goodness has not merely helpers and subordinates but mighty opponents. In the *Laws* the beneficent principle of the world is matched against an evil principle which possesses contrary powers. [*The Laws,* IV] In the *Statesman* we find it asserted that the evil principle at times prevails, and periods of universal disorder are said to alternate with orderly periods in which the divine goodness reigns without limitation or check. Plato even speaks occasionally as if matter were itself evil and responded with difficulty to the formative influence of the primal power.[10]

The conception of God warring with the evil principle is Manicheistic, one of the many indications, as some contend, of the Oriental origin of Plato's philosophy. Shelley seems to accept this Manicheism in his work prior to *Prometheus Unbound*. It is not so certain that he adheres to it therein, for his conception of evil as the creation of man, as temporal only and to be eliminated in the evolution of man as personified in Prometheus, is not wholly consistent with it. Nor is the idea that the souls seek pleasure in incarnation quite the same as the theory that they seek knowledge. Knowledge, experience of both good and evil, may be necessary to the soul's full development, to the complete wisdom which reunites it with the One.

This is apparently the belief of Plotinus, though Plotinus, as the following excerpts reveal, has several explanations.

In so far as Evil exists, the root of evil is in Matter; but Evil does not exist; all that exists, in a half-existence, is the last effort of The Good, the point at which The Good ceases because, so to speak, endlessness has all but faded out to an end. If this seem too violent a paradox . . . we must remember that it is to some degree merely metaphorical . . . it is the almost desperate effort to express a combined idea that seems to be instinctive in the mind . . . the idea that Good is all-reaching and yet that it has degrees, that an Infinitely powerful Wisdom exists and operates and casts an infinite splendor on all its works while we ourselves can see, or think we see, its failures or the last and feeblest rays of its light.[11]

Elsewhere in Plotinus are other explanations. What led the souls to forget God and encounter evil? It was due, says

[10] L. Winstanley, "Platonism in Shelley," *Essays and Studies by Members of the English Association* (Oxford, Clarendon Press, 1913), IV, 78-79.

[11] This and the succeeding excerpts are taken from the Preller-Ritter exposition and summary of Plotinus to be found in the appendix to the first volume of Stephen Mackenna's translation (London, 1917).

Plotinus, to their Rebellious Audacity, to Primal Differentiation, and to the desire of the souls to have similarly a life of their own. They began to revel in free-will, indulged in their own movement, lost the true path and forgot that they sprang from Divine Order. In love with the lower, they grew to depend on it. Human reason, Plotinus avers, is of a lower order, a human order, of understanding than the intuition:

Does the Soul employ Reasoning before it enters the body and when it has left the body, or only while it is here? Only here, where it knows doubt and care and weakness; for Intelligence is the less self-sufficing for needing to reason, just as in the crafts or arts reasoning means hesitation to the workman, but when all is plain the craft takes its own masterly way. In the Intellectual Order there is no ratiocination and the man arrived at this degree does not employ it.

But again:

. . . by the Soul's Contemplation—its zest for knowledge, its desire for experience . . . the soul, itself a Contemplation entire, has begotten another Contemplation, . . . a weaker than itself.

For, says Plotinus:

All action is in view of contemplation . . . what we have not the will-power to get by the direct way we seek by the round. When we acquire what our action sought, achieve what we proposed, what is it for? Not to be ignored but to be known, to be seen: we act for the sake of some satisfaction we desire, and this not that it may remain outside the bound of our possessions but that it may be ours. This means that it be . . . where? Where but in the mind? Thus all act circles back to thought. . . .

Again:

This lower Kosmos has been engendered not because the Divinity saw need for it, but from the sheer necessity there was for a secondary or derivative kind, since it was not in the constitution of existence that The Divine should be the latest and lowest of things.

In another passage Plotinus declares:

Vice itself is not without its usefulness to the All; it exhibits the beauty and the rightness of virtue; it calls up the intelligence to oppose the evil course; it manifests the value and grace there is in goodness by displaying the cost of sin. No doubt evil has not essentially anything to do with these purposes, but once it is there it serves in working out great ends; and only a mighty power could thus turn the ignoble to noble uses and employ to the purposes of form what has risen in formless lawlessness.

Plotinus is apparently of two or several minds on this difficult problem of evil. Sometimes he speaks as though the Soul had need of Matter, and Matter need of Soul. Sometimes it seems to be some law of necessity which leads the souls to follow their desires and seek earthly incarnation. If Shelley's doctrine of evil and its source seems somewhat ambiguous, there is justification in both Plato and Plotinus for his uncertainty.

In the passage from *Prometheus Unbound* now under consideration, Saturn, it is said, refused to "earth's primal spirits"

> The birthrights of their being, knowledge, power,
> The skill which wields the elements, the thought
> Which pierces this dim universe like light,
> Self-empire, and the majesty of love;
> For thirst of which they fainted.

Knowledge, self-empire, love, these are desired by earth's primal spirits, and this desire, if we accept another neo-Platonic doctrine, is born of Necessity. For one gathers from Plotinus that the outgoing or creative power is one of the hypostases or aspects of Deity, and that the things which Deity creates partake likewise of this need and must in turn express their being in creation. This is the outgoing or expansive function of life, as meditation is the inward or retractile function, its return to its source. The creation of Jupiter by Prometheus, the mind of man, is then a necessary act.[12]

[12] Jupiter's denial of knowledge, the birthright of their being, is an idea reminiscent of Gnosticism. Therein it is held that Sophia, subordinate min-

To the dominion of Jupiter, the gift of Prometheus, there is but one limitation: man is to be free. In this freedom lies man's only hope, for at the outset of the drama will be recalled the speech of Prometheus:

> O Mighty God!
> Almighty, had I deigned to share the shame
> Of thine ill tyranny. . . .

And again (to The Earth):

> . . . Mother, thy sons and thou
> Scorn him, without whose all-enduring will
> Beneath the fierce omnipotence of Jove,
> Both they and thou had vanished. . . .

The free creative will of man is superior to the thing which it creates, though Shelley seems to imply that it is possible for the free will to surrender its freedom by worshiping its own creation; to become subdued by religion, law, custom. Or to put the idea in the simplest terms, the mind is forever enslaved by its own previous thoughts.

Jupiter, he who reigns but who is not the Almighty nor the Merciful God, is, then, the creation of the liberated soul which, rejoicing in free will, has all but permanently enslaved itself anew—to evil not to good. And in this symbolism of Jupiter Shelley means, evidently, the deification by mankind of self-will, the individual desire to dominate at the expense of others, which manifests itself socially as tyranny, and in

---

ister of the Ultimate, the One, created the world, into which came evil personified in the earthly God, who, hating man, denied him knowledge. Sophia, however, tempted man by her genius or familiar, the snake, and man having eaten of the fruit of knowledge became cognizant of celestial things. The serpent, therefore, to the Ophist sect of the Gnostics is the saviour, not the enemy of man. Shelley's use of the serpent in the *Revolt of Islam* is congruous with this doctrine. The serpent therein symbolizes freedom and knowledge and wages eternal war with the principle of evil. That Shelley was versed in the Gnostic philosophy, as these similarities in *Prometheus Unbound* and the *Revolt of Islam* suggest, can neither be affirmed nor denied. In *The Assassins,* however, an allusion to the Gnostics supports the inference.

religion as bigotry. But so to interpret the meaning of Jupiter is perhaps somewhat to anticipate the unfolding of the argument. The picture of man's freedom in the latter scenes of the play will further illuminate the idea.

The world of Jupiter's dominion, a world of pain and misery, is the world as depicted both by Grecian and Christian mythology and as seen by the radical thought of the revolutionary philosophers who, in general, looked upon history as the record of human error. In civil and ecclesiastical institutions alike this is their finding; and their judgment Shelley apparently never questioned. In these terms Shelley depicts the tragic history of man, echoing the eloquence of Volney, and like Volney believing that notwithstanding all this evil of the past a better time was to come in which man would profit by his mistakes and mend his ways. This Utopian philosophy is manifest in Shelley's earliest writing, and though his faith in the future seems sometimes to waver, I do not recall that but for homage to the great days of Greece, the age of Plato, he has ever anything good to say of the past, save of the prophets, poets, and martyrs who kept alight the torch of hope.

The lines in the passage descriptive of man's history which are most significant of Shelley's mystical beliefs are those which depict the forces of nature as themselves infected by the evil of man's creation. Famine and disease prey upon mankind,

> . . . and the unseasonable seasons drove,
> With alternating shafts of frost and fire,
> Their shelterless, pale tribes to mountain caves.

In so depicting the physical habitat of the human species Shelley is justified by some of the scientific beliefs of his day. Erasmus Darwin had described primeval climatic conditions as superior to those of a later time; as an era with a mild cli-

mate free from storms and polar ice.[13]   Shelley apparently
attributes the change in the physical forces, their hostility to
mankind, to man himself. It is the evil in the creative mind
which produces them and it is only with the elimination of
this evil when Prometheus is freed that they are destroyed.

It is a doctrine more or less familiar to the modern world
through various cults of mental healing which describe evil
as error and as non-existent save as we think it. In the light
of neo-Platonism the modern emphasis is misleading, for to
the neo-Platonist thought is the only reality. Error indeed
will vanish as thought changes, and with it the character of
the physical world which thought creates. But it does not follow, as the cults of mental healing imply, that the change is
an easy one. Shelley, in depicting the physical characteristics
of the world man creates, is thinking in terms of neo-Platonism, to which philosophy matter is all but non-existent: is
no more than the clay from which the sculptor shapes in
visible form the images of his mental world. But in at-
tributing this power to man rather than to God, Shelley, I
think, gives to the neo-Platonic philosophy, if not a new
meaning, at least an emphasis which is new.

To the evils of man's lot, his fallen state, there are mitiga-
tions. Prometheus gives to man Hope and Love and the tools
wherewith to conquer the physical universe. This conquest
has now to be in terms of reason, for, because of his fall, that
intuitive apprehension of truth which is the mode of real being is possible to man only in flashes, is the brief reward of
the philosophic life when the soul is for a short time rapt from
its mortal state and enjoys ecstatic union with the infinite.
The way of reason is slow, laborious, evolutionary. It is in
this fashion that the methods of science and an evolutionary
theory of the physical universe are, I take it, reconciled, in

[13] *A Newton Among Poets*, p. 26.

Shelley's philosophy, with his neo-Platonic mysticism. Man's progress through reason is laborious, for it is a power which very slowly arrives at those truths which intuition grasps instantaneously.

Asia's words record the triumphs of reason, the mastery of fire and tools, the evolution of speech whereby thought is possible,[14] and the growth of science which shook "the thrones of heaven and earth." Therein lies an interesting thought. Science has threatened the God of man's creation and the political tyranny of earth. But though these powers are shaken they do not fall; knowledge alone does not suffice for complete mental freedom. That, Shelley has already shown, comes only when Prometheus foregoes hate and revenge and forgives his enemy. It is an emotional, an ethical, release, which is the necessary prelude to the liberation of his mind.

Man's progress in the arts and in medicine is depicted:

> He told the hidden power of herbs and springs,
> And Disease drank and slept. Death grew like sleep.

From its context it would seem that the last sentence referred perhaps to opiates or anodynes whereby the pain of death was softened. But there is, curiously, a passage in Shelley's early prose so similar in phrasing, though apparently of contradictory import, that Shelley may here mean something totally different.

The story of Prometheus, is one likewise which, although universally admitted to be allegorical, has never been satisfactorily explained. Prometheus stole fire from heaven, and was chained for this crime to mount Caucasus, where a vulture continually devoured his liver, that grew to meet its hunger. . . . Hesiod says, that before the time of Prometheus, mankind were exempt from suffering; that they enjoyed a vigorous youth, and that death, when at length it came, approached like sleep, and gently closed their eyes. . . . Prometheus, (who represents the human race)

[14] See p. 149, *infra.*

effected some great change in the condition of his nature, and applied fire to culinary purposes; thus inventing an expedient for screening from his disgust the horrors of the shambles. From this moment his vitals were devoured by the vulture of disease. It consumed his being in every shape of its loathsome and infinite variety, inducing the soul-quelling sinkings of premature and violent death. All vice arose from the ruin of healthful innocence. Tyranny, superstition, commerce, and inequality, were then first known, when reason vainly attempted to guide the wanderings of exacerbated passion.[15]

In his early prose passage Shelley attributes to Prometheus the introduction of cookery and the continuance of a meat diet which is the cause of all human ills. In the poem Prometheus by his wisdom allays human misery. Yet the use in both of the expression "Death grew like sleep" makes it plausible that whatever alleviation of man's bodily ills has been achieved has been through the wisdom of Prometheus and that he taught mankind (or a part of them) the merits of a vegetarian diet. The rôle of Prometheus in the two passages is precisely opposite but the cause of painless death may well be vegetarianism in both. If Shelley does not in *Prometheus Unbound* mean this, his exact implication is uncertain.

Among the gifts of Prometheus to man a knowledge of astronomy is stressed. I have elsewhere remarked on Shelley's allusions to astronomy[16] and need not, in this instance, particularize. Shelley is sketching the history of early civilizations, the astronomical lore of Egypt and Babylonia or perhaps that of some ancestral race which dwelt on the steppes of Asia north of parallel 49.[17] He celebrates the early voyages of the Phoenicians and the architectural glories of the Greeks, the beauty of whose temples in Southern Italy he so often remarks

[15] "A Vindication of Natural Diet," *Prose Works of Shelley*, ed. by Buxton Forman, 4 vols. (London, Reeves and Turner, 1880), II, 6-7.

[16] *A Newton Among Poets*, chap. X.

[17] *Ibid.*, p. 170.

in his letters[18] and to whose outdoor life he attributes their superiority in the arts.[19]

> . . . Cities then
> Were built, and through their snow-like columns flowed
> The warm winds, and the azure ether shone,
> And the blue sea and shadowy hills were seen.

But who, Asia asks, is master of Jove, who "trembled like a slave" before the curse of Prometheus. To this question Demogorgon answers:

> All spirits are enslaved which serve things evil:
> Thou knowest if Jupiter be such or no.

Asia then demands explicitly:

> Whom called'st thou God?

And to this Demogorgon replies:

> I spoke but as ye speak,
> For Jove is the supreme of living things.

It is a riddling evasion. Asia demands:

> Who is the master of the slave?

Demogorgon, forced to explicitness, replies that "the deep truth is imageless" but that to "Fate, Time, Occasion, Chance and Change"

> All things are subject but eternal love.

I find the theology of Demogorgon most intelligible in the words of Plotinus, in whose conception the Deity is a triad, whose hypostases or aspects are, that is, threefold. The first, "the One," of this triad is characterized by various synonyms of the absolute. He—or It—transcends being and we can say

---

[18] *The Letters of Percy Bysshe Shelley,* ed. by Roger Ingpen, 2 vols. (London, Sir Isaac Pitman and Sons, Ltd., 1909), II, 663 ff.
[19] *Ibid.,* p. 666.

of It only that It is not non-existent. In this concept lies the
meaning perhaps of Demogorgon's words,

> . . . Jove is the supreme of living things.

The One is more than being. Plotinus likens it to an ever-
welling spring overflowing into the lower forms of being. No
quality can be affirmed of it. It is the Transcendent, the Infinite, the Unconditioned. It is also the Good and the Beautiful. It may be thought of, therefore, as perfect Love.

The second hypostasis of the divine triad is the Universal
Intelligence which contains Ideas or Divine Thoughts, the
Real Beings. This Intelligence is productive. Accompanying
its thought is a generative principle which produces "a power
apt to the Realization of its Thought, the Third Hypostasis of
the Divine Triad." As this materialization of the Divine Ideas
proceeds of Necessity, it may be that Shelley, who evidently
conceives of Demogorgon as Necessity, the agent of the Divine
Powers, is thinking of Demogorgon as the symbol of this third
aspect of Divinity, its creative force. It is, at any rate, a ten-
tative hypothesis which I should like to advance and then later
to examine in the light of Demogorgon's subsequent rôle in
the play. In the final summing up of Shelley's philosophy this
hypothesis must be weighed.

The answer of Demogorgon that "the deep truth is imageless" and that Love is the ultimate power of the universe finds
intuitive response in Asia:

> . . . my heart gave
> The response thou hast given; and of such truths
> Each to itself must be the oracle.

This is good Platonism and neo-Platonism. Mystics of all
ages aver that the perception of truth is intuitive, not rational.
The goal of the sage and the saint is the attainment through
meditation, the trance, and rigid asceticism, of the supreme

union with God in which the Divine Reality is emotionally known. To such supreme knowledge the reason, unaided, cannot attain.

Asia's request to know the hour when

> Prometheus shall arise
> Henceforth the sun of this rejoicing world,

is answered by a vision of the "immortal Hours" among whom is one

> . . . the shadow of a destiny
> More dread than is my aspect . . .

This is the hour in which Jupiter is to be overthrown. It is succeeded by another whose beautiful chariot is symbolic of its happy destiny, the hour of the liberation of Prometheus and the beginning of a heaven on earth. These symbols are a dramatic forecast of the climax of the drama.

The description of the hours as charioteers who

> . . . with burning eyes, lean forth, and drink
> With eager lips the wind of their own speed,
> As if the thing they loved fled on before,

is clearly reminiscent of a passage in one of Shelley's letters which describes a sculptured depiction of a charioteer in similar words. The personification of the hours is reminiscent of lines in Homer and of Taylor's comment thereon previously cited. In these the hours are "winged."

> Heaven's gates spontaneous open to the powers,
> Heaven's sounding gates kept by the winged hours.

In the Spirit's song—

> My coursers are fed with the lightning,
> They drink of the whirlwind's stream,
> And when the red morning is bright'ning
> They bathe in the fresh sunbeam . . .

is introduced the symbolism of electricity which is to play so important a part in later passages of the drama. The energy and speed of the coursers is electric. The electrical energy of the atmosphere is renewed at dawn. It becomes quiescent in the middle of the day at which time the coursers rest. All this I have elsewhere argued at length.[20]

Scene v

The Spirit's song at the opening of the fifth scene reinforces the symbolism of electricity noted in the preceding scene:

> On the brink of the night and the morning
> My coursers are wont to respire.

The lines express the fact that at daybreak the atmospheric electricity is at its lowest ebb.[21]

> Their flight must be swifter than fire

is another line in keeping with this interpretation. Their speed is that of electricity.

In the prophecy of the liberating hour Asia is transformed. In Panthea's description of her she is identified with sea-born Venus:

> . . . thou didst stand
> Within a veinèd shell, which floated on
> Over the calm floor of the crystal sea,
> Among the Aegean isles. . . .

Again in Panthea's description of Asia, Love is likened to the "atmosphere of the sun's fire"—for which in physical terms may be read light, heat, and electric energy, another instance of Shelley's identification of natural and spiritual forces:

> . . . love, like the atmosphere
> Of the sun's fire filling the living world,

[20] *A Newton Among Poets,* chap. VIII.
[21] *Ibid.,* p. 131.

> Burst from thee, and illumined earth and heaven
> And the deep ocean and the sunless caves
> And all that dwell within them. . . .

The likeness of light and heat to love is a figure of natural poetic coinage. Shelley's use of it, however, is perhaps given additional weight by such a citation as the following from Swedenborg. That Shelley read Swedenborg is unknown, but his knowledge both of mystical literature and scientific literature was extensive and his acquaintance with Swedenborg is probable. The passage, in any case, is congruous with Shelley's employment of the image in *Prometheus Unbound*.

The light of heaven is not natural, as the light of the world, but it is spiritual, since it is from the Lord as the Sun, and this Sun is the Divine Love, as has been shown in the foregoing chapter. What proceeds from the Lord as the Sun is called in the heavens Divine truth, but in its essence is Divine good united to Divine truth. From this the angels have light and heat, from Divine truth light, and from Divine good heat. Hence it may be evident that the light of heaven, because from such a source, is spiritual and not natural, and likewise the heat.[22]

But to Shelley, evidently, the distinction between "spiritual" and "material" was at bottom meaningless, all things being either material or immaterial as you choose, and force one manifestation of love:

The voice in the air sings:

> Life of Life, thy lips enkindle
> With their love the breath between them;
> And thy smiles before they dwindle
> Make the cold air fire. . . .

The identification of love, light, and electric energy in this song is congruent with similar identifications elsewhere in the drama. The similarity of one image to lines in *Alastor* should be noted. In *Alastor* the lines are:

[22] Swedenborg, *Heaven and Hell* (Boston, 1883), Par. 127.

> And saw by the warm light of their own life
> Her glowing limbs beneath the sinuous veil
> Of woven wind. . . .
>
> —ll. 175-77.

In *Prometheus Unbound:*

> Child of Light! thy limbs are burning
> Through the vest which seems to hide them.

The image in both cases has additional interest in that it may be reminiscent of a poem by Sir William Jones.

Asia's song beginning

> My soul is an enchanted boat

introduces a symbol common in Shelley and one harmonious with his neo-Platonic imagery of sea, cloud, cave, and stream. On the river of individual being the soul moves as in a boat to rejoin the sea of the infinite. The symbol is frequently employed. In *Alastor* Shelley speaks of "my spirit's bark." Again in *Hellas* the bark is symbolical of Man's spirit of Will:

> For other bark than ours were needed now
> To stem the torrent of descending time.
>
> —ll. 349-50.

In *Alastor* the central image of the poem is this symbol. The neo-Platonic origin will be apparent in a passage by Synesius upon Porphyry:

> But the soul in its first descent, derives this spirit from the planetary spheres, and entering this as a boat associates itself with the corporeal world, earnestly contending that it may either at the same time draw this spirit after it, in its flight, or that they may not abide in conjunction.[22a]

Asia's song is replete with neo-Platonic symbolism. The similarity of its imagery with that of the semi-chorus in Act II,

[22a] Taylor, *Proclus,* II, 271.

scene 2 is at once apparent. In both is the association of music with generation:

> There those enchanted eddies play
> Of echoes, music-tongued, which draw,
> By Demogorgon's mighty law,
> With melting rapture, or sweet awe,
> All spirits on that secret way,
> As inland boats are driven to Ocean.

Thus Asia in her song also likens her soul to a boat

> Which, like a sleeping swan, doth float
> Upon the silver waves of thy sweet singing . . .

In one, music lures the souls into generation; in the other the soul is borne by music down the stream of life to the paradise of preëxistence. The ocean to which the soul is borne is likened to

> . . . a sea profound, of ever-spreading sound.

Is there in this employment of music as the generative cause, or as associated with it, an echo of Rosicrucianism such as Shelley may have learned in some source as yet unidentified?

The whole world is taken as a musical instrument; that is, a chromatic, sensible instrument. The common axis or pole of the world celestial is intersected—where this superior diapason or heavenly concord or chord, is divided—by the spiritual sun, or center of sentience. Every man has a little spark (sun) in his own bosom. Time is only protracted consciousness, because there is no world out of the mind conceiving it. Earthly music is the faintest tradition of the angelic state; it remains in the mind of man as the dream of, and the sorrow for, the lost paradise. Music is yet master of the man's emotions, and therefore of the man.[23]

Asia and Panthea in their journey to the cave of Demogorgon went, we have seen, back of the origins of matter and

[23] Hargrave Jennings, *The Rosicrucians, Their Rites and Doctrines,* 2 vols. (London, 1887), I, 269-70.

of generation to their source—to preëxistence, to reality. It was a philosophical quest. Asia's song which concludes the act is an emotional portrayal of the same experience. Her soul is borne by music to

> Realms where the air we breathe is love,
> Which in the winds and on the waves doth move,
> Harmonizing this earth with what we feel above.

The earth redeemed by Prometheus becomes the counterpart of heaven, the *real* universe, that of archetypes, of ideas. The philosophy therein expressed is Platonic and neo-Platonic.

But though the images are familiar they are employed in this stanza in a sense analogous to, rather than identical with, their use earlier in the poem. We find here the expression "Age's icy caves," a figure which suggests both the isolation of the individual mind, which is the familiar meaning of cave, and the greater loneliness of age. "Manhood's dark and tossing waves" suggests emotional agitation, the unhappy discords of experience of which "youth's smooth ocean, smiling to betray," is prophetic. Asia in her reversal of the soul's progress passes beyond the "glassy-gulfs" of infancy "through Death and Birth to a diviner day"; that is, to preëxistence in the world of reality. The general Platonic conception is evident enough, but Shelley here employs his symbol of the ocean in a way which asks further comment.

That the ocean is symbolical of the world of generation, we have seen from Shelley's employment of it, deriving it from the neo-Platonic imagery wherein water implies the earthly embodiment of the soul. Thence springs the symbolism of the cloud as the means of separation of the individual from the universal, and the completion of the round in the return of the individual streams to their source, the sea of universal being. In Asia's song the implication, as I understand it, is that youth, undifferentiated as yet, not yet individual, feels a false harmony with its kind. Its sense of oneness with other minds and with the universe is betrayed by the storms of life. Its separateness from its kind in maturity is symbolized by the waves which disturb the sea of being. The waves are a part of the whole and yet detached from it. They are agitated and unresting. They symbolize the unhappiness of the soul in its separation from the universal and when a prey to the storms of the emotions. In the various employments of the symbol of the ocean either as the source or the sum of being, the root significance is the same. The ocean implies unity, and any separation therefrom, whether as cloud or wave, implies the individual earthly incarnation and consequent loss of the sense of oneness with the divine.

In the latter half of the stanza, which depicts the "diviner day" of preëxistence, the symbols of water, wilderness, and sea are again employed. The "watery paths" I suppose to be, as commonly in Shelley's employment of the symbol, the streams of individual experience. The "wildernesses calm and green" are the universe outside of the individual percipient which promises experience to the soul. They in their celestial fashion, though "calm and bright," are analogous to the external world of earthly experience, the source of bodily sensation. Wilderness in both cases is the symbol of that which separates the individual soul from the universal, the One, the homogeneous unity symbolized in the sea.

The sea, it will be noted, is employed again in the last line of the song. The bright shapes which people the wildernesses of paradise "walk upon the sea, and chant melodiously." Is there here some distinction between the paradise to which Asia's soul has returned and the sea of universal mind or spirit upon which walk the bright shapes, if this be the meaning of "sea" in this instance? I believe such a distinction is meant and that it is one in accord both with neo-Platonic beliefs and with the Oriental philosophy whence those beliefs presumably derive.

Nirvana, in the Oriental concept, the union of the individual soul with the One, with God, is the ultimate reward of the good, but is to be attained only after many earthly incarnations. Between these incarnations the soul, according to its deserts, spends an interval of varying duration either in Hell or in one of the various paradises. In its ascent to Nirvana, the reincarnations of the soul and its respites in Paradise may be very many before its attainment of eternal bliss wherein it is forever exempt from mortality. Paradise is, in this conception, not an eternal but a transitory phase of the soul's journey; nor despite the joys which it gives does it wholly satisfy.

This concept is in modern thought familiar in the doctrines of Theosophy which derive it presumably from Hindoo and neo-Platonic sources. For the idea is to be found also in neo-Platonism. The stay of the souls in the fields of asphodel or in the heaven of the Milky Way is not eternal. They are lured to earthly incarnation, return to their reward or punishment, and ultimately, after aeons, may attain their timeless union with the One. Such is the belief which a reading of the last stanza of Asia's song makes probable. Shelley must have been familiar with it in the literature of neo-Platonism and in that of Indian philosophy—the latter in part through the writings of Sir William Jones.

PROMETHEUS UNBOUND: ACT III

In the opening lines of Act III Jupiter bids the heavenly host rejoice at his impending omnipotence:

> . . . alone
> The soul of man, like unextinguished fire,
> Yet burns towards heaven with fierce reproach, and doubt,
> And lamentation and reluctant prayer,
> Hurling up insurrection, which might make
> Our antique empire insecure, though built
> On eldest faith, and hell's coeval, fear.

Despite the oppressions of this trinity of faith, hell, and fear, the soul of man has climbed the crags of life—

> It yet remains supreme o'er misery,
> Aspiring, unrepressed, yet soon to fall.

The means to man's overthrow, his complete subjection, Jupiter then describes.

Jupiter characterizes his new creation as "a strange wonder," as "that fatal child, the terror of the earth," a monster which, at the "destined hour" is to bear "the dreadful might of ever-living limbs" from the vacant throne of Demogorgon. If Demogorgon is, as we have been led to believe from our previous analysis, the creative spirit in Nature operating of necessity, then the monster of Jupiter's begetting is to usurp the power of Necessity and man thenceforth is to be forever enslaved. For the Necessity which is one hypostasis of the Divine and subject only to Love, is to be substituted another Necessity born of Jupiter and "Thetis, bright image of eternity."

In obvious symbolism Thetis, sea-nymph, is the image of eternity as the sea is the mirror of the heavens. This, however, is a superficial reading only. The marriage of Jupiter to Thetis is to symbolize the eternity of his reign. Jupiter's tenure has hitherto been uncertain but is now to endure, and this through the creation of the strange wonder which Jupiter has begotten of Thetis:

> Two mighty spirits, mingling, made a third
> Mightier than either, which, embodied now,
> Between us floats, felt although unbeheld.
> Waiting the incarnation, which ascends
> . . . from Demogorgon's throne.

Jupiter has begotten of the image of Eternity a spirit mightier than either which is to become incarnate with the might of Demogorgon, of Necessity. The meaning seems to be that for the old form of Necessity, in which a degree of freedom remained to the soul of man, is to be substituted another, one fatal to man which will

> . . . redescend and trample out the spark.

The spark is man's resistance, his will to endure.

Thetis and her part in this symbolism may be made more intelligible perhaps by this passage from Plotinus: "Time is not a piece snipped from eternity, and measured out—it is the image of Eternity; Eternity made visible."[1] If Shelley had some such neo-Platonic idea in mind, Thetis may be thought of as time defined as "an image of Eternity" and her union with Jupiter as symbolical of the extension of Jupiter's power throughout time.

Jupiter mistakenly believes that time may be prolonged to become, indeed, eternity. In this self-deception and his marriage to Thetis he embraces but a shadow. For time is an unreality, the phantom image of eternity, and must ultimately

---

[1] Charles Bigg, *Neo-Platonism* (E. and J. B. Young and Company, New York, 1895), p. 211.

yield to the necessity of the Eternal One embodied in Demogorgon. Hence, at last, comes the inevitable overthrow of Jupiter when Time is "borne to his tomb in Eternity." For Jupiter, being the creation of man before man's union with the One, the timeless, can himself exist only in time. Demogorgon describes himself as "Eternity, demand no direr name" and declares further to Jupiter,

> I am thy child as thou wert Saturn's child.

Time, then, is the issue or shadow of Eternity. But Eternity likewise is the issue of Time, for Time is necessarily succeeded by Eternity in that it is less than Eternity.

The difficulty of the symbolism inherent in Jupiter and Demogorgon is not, however, so easily solved if our desire is to understand Shelley's conception of Necessity in the scheme of things, for Necessity is of a twofold aspect, that which may be called scientific Necessity, celebrated in *Queen Mab,* and that which is the theme of Platonic and neo-Platonic speculation. The two are not the same, and Shelley's philosophic progress is marked by a surrender of the ideas which he announces in *Queen Mab* and the substitution therefor of the more difficult but philosophically more acceptable concept of Plato and Plotinus.

In *Queen Mab* Shelley apostrophizes

> Spirit of Nature! all-sufficing Power,
> Necessity! thou mother of the world!
> —VI, ll. 197-98.

The deities of the French Revolutionary philosophers were Necessity and Reason. Nor is it difficult to see why. Belief in Necessity was, in the phenomenal world, belief in law; each effect must have its cause. Exceptions to the reign of law were impossible. Therefore claims made by religion to such exceptions, such departures from strict causation, were unwarranted in fact and were evidence of superstition. The battle over Necessity was a battle between the scientific and the traditionally religious ways of interpreting the universe. It was the more bitter in that ecclesiasticism had thwarted science and, as the Revolutionary philosophers believed, debased mankind. Therefore it was a commonplace of radical belief that the human reason could liberate mankind only as man discarded all superstition, all belief that natural law could ever be violated.

In his notes to *Queen Mab*[2] Shelley cites with approval a passage from the high-priest of Necessitarianism, Holbach, to the effect that the place of every particle of dust in a whirlwind is determined by precedent facts, and that in social revolutions every action, word, and desire of every participant is likewise predetermined. The mechanistic philosophy could have no more rigid and absolute expression. It is eloquent and poetic, and the youthful Shelley was charmed by it as being an admirable weapon wherewith to slay the illogicalities and absurdities of religion.

But there is a flaw concealed within it for one who worshiped the reign of law in the universe and who wished at the same time very materially to alter in that universe a number of things which were not to his liking. If everything is predetermined including every thought and desire of every human being, how then can anything be altered save as preëxisting causes permit? If a man is no more than a machine, wherein is he free to alter himself or others? In practise, of course, no man believes himself a machine. He believes that he can think as he wishes and in part do as he pleases. He acts tacitly on that belief, and no matter what his abstract philosophy may be, attempts to reform the world. Therefore we find the youthful Shelley while subscribing to the doctrine of

[2] Note to VI, ll. 171-73.

Necessity yet ardently seeking to reconstruct society through the exercise of the human reason.

The youthful Shelley is clearly inconsistent, avowing one faith while acting on quite contrary, if unconscious, assumptions. Yet he is not alone in his ambiguity, for "necessitarians," as they appear in one age and another under whatsoever name and guise, are accustomed, like Shelley, to deny the philosophical possibility of freedom while in effect enjoying it themselves and assuming it in others. The discrepancy here is between theory and practise, between intellectual belief and emotional belief. Either there is some confusion in words which asks more accurate definition of the terms "necessity" and "free will"; or those terms are employed philosophically in too absolute a sense. Perhaps the age-long conflict between free will and necessity is due to the fact that neither is wholly true: man may be partly free and partly bound.

That Shelley's position with regard to free will *vs.* determinism is not wholly unambiguous is I think evident from a study of his prose and verse. But it is likewise true that he confesses in his later prose the complete inadequacy of materialism and the necessitarianism implicit in that faith. These excerpts from his prose will make the point clear:

We live and move and think; but we are not the creators of our own origin and existence. We are not the arbiters of every motion of our own complicated nature; we are not the masters of our own imaginations and moods of mental being. There is a Power by which we are surrounded, like the atmosphere in which some motionless lyre is suspended, which visits with its breath our silent chords at will.

Our most imperial and stupendous qualities—those on which the majesty and power of humanity is erected—are, relatively to the inferior portion of its mechanism, active and imperial; but they are the passive slaves of some higher and more omnipotent Power. This Power is God; and those who have seen God have, in the period of their purer and more perfect nature, been harmonized by their own will to so excellent a consentaneity of power as to give forth divinest melody, when the breath of universal being sweeps over their frame.[3]

In the foregoing passage Shelley's doctrine closely resembles that of Plotinus who believes in the freedom of the will but "denies that it can effect things mutually contradictory." Free will is shown in right action. When acting evilly it is not free. "Only when our soul acts by its native pure and independent Reason-Principle can the act be described as ours and as an exercise of Free-Will." Plotinus contends that the liberty by which we accomplish evil is the negation of freedom, an idea which Demogorgon voices:

> All spirits are enslaved which serve things evil;
> Thou knowest if Jupiter be such or no.
> —II, iv, 110-11.

In another passage Shelley remarks on the external resemblances and internal differences of men:

None is exempt, indeed, from that species of influence which affects, as it were, the surface of his being, and gives the specific outline to his conduct. Almost all that is ostensible submits to that legislature created by the general representation of the past feelings of mankind—imperfect as it is from a variety of causes, as it exists in the government, the religion, and domestic habits. Those who do not nominally, yet actually, submit to the same power. The external features of their conduct, indeed, can no more escape it, than the clouds can escape from the stream of the wind; and his opinion, which he often hopes he has dispassionately secured from all contagion of prejudice and vulgarity, would be found, on examination, to be the inevitable excrescence of the very usages from which he vehemently dissents. Internally all is conducted otherwise; the efficiency, the essence, the vitality of actions, derives its colour from what is no ways contributed to it from any

[3] "Essay on Christianity," in *Essays and Letters*, ed. by Ernest Rhys (London, Walter Scott, 1887), p. 87.

external source. Like the plant, which while it derives the accident of its size and shape from the soil in which it springs, and is cankered, or distorted, or inflated, yet retains those qualities which essentially divide it from all others; so that hemlock continues to be poison, and the violet does not cease to emit its odour in whatever soil it may grow.

We consider our own nature too superficially. We look on all that in ourselves with which we can discover a resemblance in others; and consider those resemblances as the materials of moral knowledge. It is in the differences that it actually consists.[4]

There is evident in this passage the wish to insure individual moral freedom in a world which in externals is deterministic. In another place Shelley openly disavows the materialism which he had so eloquently praised in *Queen Mab:*

It is a decision against which all our persuasions struggle, and we must be long convicted before we can be convinced that the solid universe of external things is "such stuff as dreams are made of." The shocking absurdities of the popular philosophy of mind and matter, its fatal consequences in morals, and their violent dogmatism concerning the source of all things, had early conducted me to materialism. This materialism is a seducing system to young and superficial minds. It allows its disciples to talk and dispenses them from thinking. But I was discontented with such a view of things as it afforded; man is a being of high aspirations, "looking both before and after," whose "thoughts wander through eternity," disclaiming alliance with transcience and decay; incapable of imagining to himself annihilation; existing but in the future and the past; being not what he is, but what he has been and will be. Whatever may be his true and final destination, there is a spirit within him at enmity with nothingness and dissolution.[5]

A passage from a letter written but a few months before Shelley's death is further evidence of his recantation and,

---

[4] "Speculations in Morals," *ibid.,* p. 135.
[5] "On Life," *ibid.,* p. 73.

incidentally, of his unchanging hostility towards institutional Christianity:

I differ with Moore in thinking Christianity useful to the world; no man of sense can think it true; and the alliance of the monstrous superstitions of the popular worship with the pure doctrines of the Theism of such a man as Moore, turns to the profit of the former, and makes the latter the fountain of its own pollution. I agree with him, that the doctrines of the French, and Material Philosophy, are as false as they are pernicious; but still they are better than Christianity, inasmuch as anarchy is better than despotism; for this reason, that the former is for a season, and the latter is eternal.[6]

These passages offer a clear disavowal of the materialistic philosophy which Shelley had so enthusiastically endorsed as a disciple of Holbach. "Necessity" does not, however, vanish with it from the scene. The Platonism or neo-Platonism of Shelley's later belief does not deny Necessity a place in the scheme of things. What the doctrine of Plotinus was has been indicated. It is ambiguous, to the effect that the enfranchised spirit is free to do only what is right. In the choice of earthly good or evil the human soul seeking this enfranchisement has, apparently, some freedom; an increasingly greater freedom as it escapes from sensual toils; less freedom as it abandons itself to sensual pleasures.

Plato's philosophy likewise, in his conception of a world soul, finds a subordinate place for mechanical necessity. In the realm of sensation and materialism, mechanical necessity is responsible for the imperfections of the material world and runs counter to the higher principle. The "ideas" or archetypes of the world of "reality" are, because of this lower or mechanical necessity, but imperfectly realized. Shelley, therefore, in his philosophical evolution from Holbach to Plato and the neo-Platonists was not called upon wholly to discard his belief

[6] Letter to Horace Smith, April 11, 1822. Ingpen, II, 959.

in Necessity. Rather this belief assumes a subordinate place, acquires a different emphasis. The conflict between Demogorgon and the "Mighty Spirit" created by Jupiter and Thetis is, as I understand it, a conflict between that Necessity which is the creative agent of God, and the scientific Necessity of man's invention with which he is in danger of enslaving himself.

That Shelley perceived the danger of such an enslavement his prose disclaimer of materialism declares. If my interpretation is correct, the symbolism of *Prometheus Unbound* likewise declares it. It is the faith of Prometheus that he shall some day be freed and Jupiter overthrown; but it is he who really frees himself by casting out hate. By this exercise of moral freedom he becomes, then, in harmony with the principle of Love and thenceforth is master of Necessity, not its victim. For, says Demogorgon, "Fate, Time, Occasion, Chance, and Change" are subject only to eternal Love.

The Necessity which Jupiter hopes to fasten upon man and with which he thinks to usurp the might of Demogorgon exists in time. With this, as symbolized in his marriage with Thetis, Jupiter expects to supplant eternity. But such an usurpation is impossible unless man enslaves himself to his own thought and denies the freedom of his will. Provided his will remains firm, the tyranny of the God whom he has created must sometime end. Man must, or at any rate does, free himself from his own miscreation. The implication seems to be that the self-conquest of Prometheus and his growth in the power to choose is a process all but infinitely long, though in the end achieved. The freeing of the will seems, too, to depend upon an ethical choice. Renunciation of hatred, the growth in Prometheus of the spirit of love, is necessary to the enfranchisement of mind and will. Thenceforth Prometheus can think only good, for he has attained union with the One. In the One, who is timeless, Jupiter, who can exist only in time, has no place. In vain he lifts his lightnings. He calls upon the world to fall in ruins upon himself and his enemy. The elements obey him not and he sinks into the abyss, conquered by Demogorgon, that Necessity which is the agent of the One, of divine love. The necessitarian God (Jupiter) of man's creation, who can exist only in time, is destroyed by the God of Love, who is timeless. In this catastrophe there is Necessity also, personified in Demogorgon, but Necessity on a different plane of thought.

In the scene descriptive of Jupiter's overthrow, scientific symbolism parallels the neo-Platonic symbolism. The lightnings which Jupiter vainly seeks to wield are energy withdrawn from its legitimate and beneficent ends and turned to destructive ends. Electricity in its peaceful round of duties is necessary to the creation of life, to the formation of clouds, to rainfall, and the growth of plants. In the hands of Jupiter it is lightning, the destroyer. Prometheus, when he displaces Jupiter, becomes master of the elements and directs the energy of the universe to his own beneficent creations.

SCENE II

The second scene of the act is a dialogue between Ocean and Apollo in which is described the final passage of the conflict between Jupiter and Demogorgon. The peace which is henceforth to rule the world is symbolically depicted in the "Heaven-reflecting sea," tempestuous once when the heavens were at war but now hungering for the azure calm which is fed to it from the urns which stand beside Neptune's throne. The sea is presumably symbolical of matter:

"Again according to Plato, the deep, the sea, and a tempest are so many symbols of the constitution of matter."[7] Shelley, as we have seen, employs it also as a symbol for generation,

[7] Taylor, *Proclus*, II, 294.

the sum of all being as of matter. Yet matter and being are really one, are but forms of the one divine energy. The sea then symbolizes unity, whether of matter or of being. The urns which stand beside Neptune's throne and from which the sea is fed with calm are reminiscent in their imagery of another passage to be found in Taylor's *Proclus:*

> Two urns by Jove's high throne have ever stood
> The source of evil one, and one of good.

If the sea is to be thought of in this instance as symbolical of matter, the peace which comes upon it symbolizes the new reign of love. The "many-peopled continents" and the "fortunate isles" are emblems of man's peaceful life under the new order. Yet necessity remains the law of material things, though these no longer oppress man and, as later appears, he is master of them.

> The floating bark of the light-laden moon
> With that white star, its sightless pilot's crest.

The "sightless pilot" is Destiny as we learn from Shelley's employment of the same image in *Hellas:*

> The world's eyeless charioteer,
> Destiny, is hurrying by!
> —l. 712.

and again,

> Art thou eyeless like old Destiny?
> —l. 121.

The meaning in all is evidently the same. But man newly liberated is master of material destiny. Law rules the universe of things but man is above the law, for in his knowledge, his science, he turns the laws of matter to his own ends. The higher and the lower Necessity has each its proper sphere and function, but man in his identification with the higher Neces-

sity becomes master of the lower. Is this a mere juggling of
words and terms? It is, at any rate, in accord with the distinctions of the Platonic philosophy. The soul, itself a contemplation, produces in its zest for knowledge, its desire for
experience, another contemplation weaker than itself, the
Kosmós.

Important among the themes of meditation which are to
occupy Prometheus in his cave are the ideas of beauty to which
the arts give sensible form:

> And lovely apparitions,—dim at first
> Then radiant, as the mind, arising bright
> From the embrace of beauty (whence the forms
> Of which these are the phantoms) casts on them
> The gathered rays which are reality—
> Shall visit us, the progeny immortal
> Of Painting, Sculpture, and rapt Poesy,
> And Arts, though unimagined, yet to be.
> The wandering voices and the shadows these
> Of all that man becomes, the mediators
> Of that best worship love, by him and us
> Given and returned; swift shapes and sounds which grow
> More fair and soft as man grows wise and kind,
> And, veil by veil, evil and error fall.

This emphasis upon the importance of Beauty and the arts is
rather of neo-Platonic than Platonic origin.[8] In Plato, of the
absolute qualities identifiable with the One, the Good is most
stressed, although Beauty is another of its transcendent attributes. Ethically it is the good life, the socially good life,
which most concerns Plato. Philosopher and statesman rank
highest in his hierarchy, and his characterizations even of

---

[8] "All the productions of nature or art are the works of a certain wisdom
which ever presides over their creation. Art is made possible only by the
existence of this wisdom. The talent of the artist is derived from the wisdom
of nature which presides over the production of every work." Plotinus, V, 8,
5, in *Complete Works,* trans. by Kenneth S. Guthrie, 4 vols. (London, G.
Bell and Sons, 1918), II, 559.

poets are somewhat condescending. They are, seemingly, falsifiers, however pleasing.

In Plotinus, although the Good remains the attribute of Deity most stressed, Beauty is more emphatically than in Plato identified with the One, as is evident in the following excerpt:

The Power which resides in the intelligible world is pure "being," but perfectly beautiful "being." Without beauty, what would become of "being"? Without "being," what would become of beauty? "Being" itself would be annihilated by the beauty of "being." "Being" is therefore desirable, it is identical with beauty, and beauty is amiable because it is "being." Seeing that both are of the same nature, it would be useless to inquire which is the principle of the other. The deceptive "being" (of bodies) needs to receive the image borrowed from beauty to appear beautiful; and in general, to exist; it exists only in so far as it participates in the beauty found in "being"; the greater its participation, the more perfect is it, because it appropriates this beautiful being all the more.[9]

Beauty, in this sense, is the intellectual beauty praised in Shelley's hymn. The work of the artist is necessarily an imperfect shadow of this divine beauty, as Asia is the shadow of a greater loveliness. Nevertheless Plotinus seemingly places a greater value upon the arts than does Plato, among them music being first.

The musician allows himself to be easily moved by beauty, and admires it greatly; but he is not able by himself to achieve the intuition of the beautiful. He needs the stimulation of external impressions. Just as some timorous being is awakened by the least noise, the musician is sensitive to the beauty of the voice and of harmonies. He avoids all that seems contrary to the laws of harmony and of unity, and enjoys rhythm and melodies in instrumental and vocal music. After these purely sensual intonations, rhythm and tunes, he will surely in them come to distinguish form from matter, and to contemplate the beauty existing in their proportions and relations. He will have to be taught that what excites

[9] *Idem.,* V, 8, 9 (Guthrie, II, 566).

his admiration in these things, is their intelligible harmony, the beauty it contains, and, in short, beauty absolute, and not particular. He will have to be introduced to philosophy by arguments that will lead him to recognize truths that he ignored, though he possessed them instinctively.[10]

Again, in the next excerpt, Plotinus declares that beauty in an art work is of divine origin, an intuition of the artist, and suggests that in the practise of his art he raises himself beyond the beauty which resides in exterior objects and approaches the divine.

Since he who rises to the contemplation of the intelligible world, and who conceives the beauty of true intelligence, can also, as we have pointed out by intuition grasp the superior Principle, the Father of Intelligence, let us, so far as our strength allows us, try to understand and explain to ourselves how it is possible to contemplate the beauty of Intelligence and of the intelligible world. Let us imagine two pieces of marble placed side by side, the one rough and inartistic, the other one fashioned by the sculptor's chisel, who made of it the statue of a goddess, a grace, or a muse; or that of a man—but not that of any individual whatever, but that of a (cultured gentle) man in whom art would have gathered all the traits of beauty offered by different individuals. After having thus from art received the beauty of the form, the second marble will appear beautiful, not by virtue of its essence, which is to be stone—for otherwise the other block would be as beautiful as this one—but because of the form received through art. The latter, however, did not exist in the matter of the statue. It was in the thought of the artist that it existed before passing into the marble; and it existed therein, not because it had eyes and hands, but because it participated in art. It was therefore in art that this superior beauty existed. . . . As the nature of art is to produce beauty, if art succeed in producing beauty which conforms to its constitutive essence, then, by the possession of the beauty essential to it, art possesses a beauty still greater and truer than that which passes into exterior objects.[11]

[10] *Idem*, I, 3, 1 (Guthrie, I, 270).
[11] *Idem.*, V, 8, 1 (Guthrie, II, 551).

Because of its possible relation to Shelley, or its derivation from the same source, it may be worth noting that Keats's aesthetic philosophy of beauty as truth resembles both the doctrine of Plotinus and Shelley's thought as expressed in the *Defence of Poetry*. Keats, like Shelley, glorifies the function of the poet and reiterates in his letters and his verse that "What the imagination seizes as Beauty must be Truth."[12] The souls in this "vale of soul-making," as he called the world, find their salvation in their aesthetic progress from the physical pleasures to the delights of music, and ultimately friendship and love.[13] *Endymion* symbolically depicts such a progress from a lower to a higher love.

The thought derives ultimately from neo-Platonism, but Keats may have got it from some English paraphrase of the transcendental philosophy current in his day in Germany. Henry Crabb Robinson writing from Germany in 1802 declares:

Understanding is considered by the New School as a very subordinate faculty. . . . Poetry and Mysticism these are the Idols worshipped here—Beauty and Truth are asserted to be one—Poetry is maintained to be nothing but esoteric philosophy and Philosophy esoteric poetry!!! . . .[14]

A very few excerpts from Shelley's *Defence of Poetry* will suggest the similarity of his beliefs to those of Keats and to the new philosophy of Germany, especially the moral importance which he ascribes to poetry as a mediator between man and the divine:

Poetry is ever found to co-exist with whatever other arts contribute to the happiness and perfection of man.[15]

[12] Albert Elmer Hancock, *John Keats* (Boston and New York, Houghton Mifflin and Company, 1908), p. 63.

[13] *Ibid.,* p. 64.

[14] *Crabb Robinson in Germany (1800-1805). Extracts from His Correspondence,* ed. by Edith J. Morley (Oxford, 1929), p. 14.

[15] In *Essays and Letters* (ed. by Rhys), p. 14.

Poetry, and the principle of Self, of which money is the visible incarnation, are the God and Mammon of the world.[16]

What were virtue, love, patriotism, friendship—what were the scenery of this beautiful universe which we inhabit; what were our consolations on this side of the grave—and what were our aspirations beyond it, if poetry did not ascend to bring light and fire from those eternal regions where the owl-winged faculty of calculation dare not soar?[17]

Poets are the hierophants of an unapprehended inspiration; the mirrors of the gigantic shadows which futurity casts upon the present; the words which express what they understand not; the trumpets which sing to battle, and feel not what they inspire; the influence which is moved not, but moves. Poets are the unacknowledged legislators of the world.[18]

Shelley, as is to be expected of a poet, magnifies the importance of poetry and of the other arts, even those which "though unimagined" are yet to be. Art is elevated to an equality with philosophy, and the way of the artist becomes like that of saint and philosopher an approach to divinity. These aesthetic implications, at best latent in Plato, are given greater emphasis by Plotinus, and reach their full expression in Keats and in Shelley. That the growth of Shelley's aesthetic philosophy received an impetus from the transcendental philosophy of contemporary Germany, itself deriving from neo-Platonism, seems likely enough; but what specific works may have influenced him I do not know.[18a] To identify them, though of considerable potential interest in itself, is not essential to an understanding of *Prometheus Unbound,* Plotinus and Plato, Shelley's identifiable sources, sufficing for that purpose. Near the end of the passage descriptive of the arts which are to entertain Prometheus in his cave occurs the line,

And, veil by veil, evil and error fall.

[16] *Ibid.,* p. 33.   [17] *Ibid.,* p. 34.   [18] *Ibid.,* p. 40.
[18a] Schiller's early verse, however, is in several instances notably neo-Platonic.

That evil and error obscure the divine reality which is at the heart of life is the evident meaning of the passage and harmonious with the belief, whether Oriental or neo-Platonic, that earthly life is one of illusion. The word "veil" itself and Shelley's symbolical employment of it ask a passing comment, however, for like "shadow" its implications are mystical. In the song in Act II, scene 5, descriptive of Asia she is said to be hidden by the radiance of her beauty:

> And this atmosphere divinest
> Shrouds thee whereso'er thou shinest.

"Shroud" in this instance is a synonym for the more customary "veil." The figure elsewhere occurs as in *Hellas:*

> . . . climes where now, veiled by the ardor of day
> Thou art hidden . . .
>
> —ll. 1043-44.

And again in *Hellas:*

> Like orient mountains lost in day.
>
> —l. 85.

That death or life may be thought of as veiling reality appears in such an instance as this in *Adonais:*

> And death is a low mist which cannot blot
> The brightness it may veil.
>
> —ll. 391-92.

In the speech of the Earth which shortly follows the long description by *Prometheus* of the cave and its joys of meditation and creation (scene 3) occurs a similar employment of the figure in the oft quoted lines:

> Death is the veil which those who live call Life:
> They sleep, and it is lifted.

Scene III

Strength, says Hercules, making obeisance to Prometheus, ministers "like a slave"

To wisdom, courage, and long-suffering love.

Shelley repeats in this the law earlier pronounced by Demogorgon, that Love is the ultimate power of the universe. The words of Prometheus to Asia are likewise in accord with neo-Platonism:

> Asia, thou light of life,
> Shadow of beauty unbeheld.

The earthly Venus is said by neo-Platonism to be the worldly counterpart of the divine love. "Shadow" is here employed in a characteristic Shelleyan and neo-Platonic sense. The union of Prometheus and Asia, that is of the mind of man and of the forces of love and creation, is now reëstablished and in that union are incorporated the "fair sister nymphs" Panthea and Ione, who, if our reading is correct, symbolize sympathy and the love of beauty. All these loves are henceforth to be one in the mind of man.

The symbol of the cave reappears, implying the subjective life of the Promethean age in which mind is forever to contemplate love and beauty. In the cave the fountain, source of divine inspiration, of spiritual intuition, has its accustomed place. And in the serenity and unchangeableness of this contemplative life there is contentment and stability, despite the mutability of human things.

What can hide man from mutability? The idea, seemingly, is that the social mind, mankind as a whole, is happy and eternal although the individual, the human mortal, is subject to the vicissitudes of change. Ione, in keeping with her symbolic rôle, chants "the fragments of sea-music," music of divine inspiration, the sea being the symbol of the universal or divine mind. It is with this and kindred aesthetic employments that the Mind of Man is to beguile the eternity of its bliss.

The passage is wholly neo-Platonic. To the cave of mind—
to contemplation—come

> The echoes of the human world, which tell
> Of the low voice of love, almost unheard,
> And dove-eyed pity's murmured pain, and music,
> Itself the echo of the heart, and all
> That tempers or improves man's life, now free.

For the end of earthly experience is to provide the soul with
the materials for reflection. In the divine Triad itself there is,
besides the ineffable source of all, the dual function of creation
and contemplation; and the human soul, a lesser counterpart
of the divine, in its outgoing aspect is creative, but in its contemplative aspect seeks its reunion with God, meditating upon
the experiences of earthly life. It is this need of experience
which, in Plotinus, is the necessity which determines the incarnation of souls.

All action is in view of contemplation. . . . What we have not
the will-power to get by the direct way we seek by the round.
When we acquire what our action sought, achieve what we proposed, what is it for? Not to be ignored but to be known, to be
seen: we act for the sake of some satisfaction we desire, and this
not that it may remain outside the bound of our possessions but
that it may be ours. This means that it be—where? Where but
in the mind? Thus all act circles back to thought, for what the
act lays up in the soul, which is a Reason-Principle, can be nothing
else than a Reason-Form, a silent thought (a thought not marred
by the noise of action.)[19]

In this instance life and the waking state are likened to death
and sleep in that they are barriers to the true life of the soul
which is elsewhere. Death and sleep are, in reality, the way
to the free life of the spirit disengaged from mortal coils. The
figure, which curiously inverts the usual meaning of the

---

[19] Plotinus, III, 85 (Mackenna).

words, is in accord with mystical beliefs and its employment by Shelley is evidence of his preoccupation with them.

The reader of *Prometheus Unbound* comes, with reason, to suspect a double meaning in every line and a symbol in every image. Thus the "mystic shell" whose "mighty music" Ione is to loosen may bear some symbolic interpretation. That Ione is to be the herald of the new day is congruous with her function as we have interpreted it. The shell, too, has associations with the sea, symbol sometimes of matter, sometimes of the universal mind from which souls are born and to which they return. In a conch shell, moreover, lingers the echo of the sea. It is a poetic instrument for its purpose therefore, in this instance, but I detect no more explicit symbolism in its employment than I have mentioned.

The speech of the Earth which follows asks more comment, for the thought is in its character commingled of scientific and mystical implications. The earth feels through her "withered, old, and icy frame" "the warmth of an immortal youth." I take the passage to mean, first, that in the Promethean day all life, all nature, are magically renewed and that, secondly, this renewal is to be conceived of in the terms of natural science as the consequence of greater heat and electric energy. I need not repeat here the arguments and analogies drawn from science which I have elsewhere discussed.[20] In brief the conclusion is that the mephitic gases of the earth, "the poison of despair" and source of "disease and pain," become health giving. That gases are explicitly meant is evident from the passage which refers to the oracles and the madness which seized upon the worshipers. The oracles thus inspired

. . . lured
The erring nations round to mutual war.

[20] *A Newton Among Poets*, p. 189.

The breath of earth, the spirit which was "panted forth in anguish," is now as "a violet's exhalation." This gas, "a crimson air," feeds the vine and the ivy. That it is identifiable with nitrous oxide, incredible as such an identification may seem at first sight, is to my mind certain from the importance of the gas in the scientific experimentation of Shelley's time, and even more conclusively from a passage in Erasmus Darwin, similar in phrasing and avowedly descriptive of this gas.[21]

A few lines prior to the Earth's discussion of the oracle and the "crimson air" occurs the passage in which are the lines previously mentioned:

> Death is the veil which those who live call life:
> They sleep, and it is lifted.

That this is neo-Platonic in implication is evident. Asia has asked the meaning of death:

> Cease they to love, and move, and breathe, and speak,
> Who die?

The Earth in answer says:

> It would avail not to reply:
> Thou art immortal, and this tongue is known
> But to the uncommunicating dead.

And thereupon death is likened to a veil. The passage has interest as expressing, in part, Shelley's views upon immortality. The question is rather too big a one to be debated here and rather than cite variously from numerous poems and prose passages I shall state what I believe to be a justifiable conclusion: (1) that in his poetry Shelley more explicitly states his belief in personal immortality than he does in his prose; (2) that in his poetry the expressions of his belief become less

[21] *Ibid.*, p. 190.

ambiguous and more numerous in his later work than in the earlier. There are apparent reasons for these conclusions.

In his essays, notes, and prose fragments Shelley is dialectical; his one instrument is the reason. That he was a keen debater is evident in his *Necessity of Atheism,* his essays, and many of his letters. In these he is not the poet but the philosopher and controversialist. But in his poetry a wider range of powers is called for. Not only the reason but intuitions have there a legitimate place. The longing for a richer life in a happier world is a partial justification for belief in it, and the intuitive sense that the self is eternal suffices for faith. To this may be added Shelley's growing interest in the Platonic philosophy, for which, both in Plato and the neo-Platonists, the eternal existence of the soul not only subsequent to, but prior to, earthly incarnation, is a fundamental tenet. Shelley in his last four years, the years of his great poetry, is, at least with the poetical part of him, however reason may demur, a believer in some form of survival; though it may be argued that this belief, if it is in the reunion of the individual soul with the All-Soul, or Nirvana, may be thought of as not strictly a *personal* survival, but the loss of personality in the One. Shelley's conception of this union stresses rather the enrichment of personality, its heightened expression in the arts and sciences. All mankind is to be one in goodness but disparate in its individual self-expression. It is not life which Shelley wishes to escape but the thwarted imperfect life of humanity as it now is. With the freeing of Prometheus life is to be enriched. Man, though good, is not to be passionless. At one with his kind he is yet to be more truly individual than before.

At the end of the Earth's speech prior to the summoning of the Spirit of the Earth mention is made of an earthly cave which now is the source of beneficent instead of noxious gases.

"This cave," says the Earth to Prometheus, "is thine." Dramatically speaking there is here, surely, a redundancy of caves, and it is only as "cave" is symbolically interpreted that the word is intelligible. This interpretation can be made without casuistry, if we remember that a cave in neo-Platonic and Shelleyan symbolism implies the earth, earthly existence, the soul in its isolation, or the habitation of soul (as in the cave of Demogorgon). In the present instance I take it to mean that the Earth surrenders this cavern whence her spirit "was panted forth in anguish" and which now is the source of beneficent forces, as a symbol of the surrender to Demogorgon of the forces of nature, of material energy, which he, not Jupiter, henceforth is to wield.

That this is the probable meaning of the symbol is strengthened by the Earth's summoning of the Spirit of the Earth.

> This is my torch-bearer,
> Who let his lamp out in old time with gazing
> On eyes from which he kindled it anew
> With love, which is as fire, sweet daughter mine,
> For such is that within thine own.

The identification of the Spirit of the Earth with electricity, and the further identification of electric energy with Love, from this and other passages, I have elsewhere demonstrated at length and need not here repeat.[22] It is, happily, the least disputable of the scientific readings of Shelley's symbolism. The Spirit of the Earth, symbol of energy, is reunited now with Asia, the Spirit of Love in Nature. The Cave of its habitation is surrendered to Prometheus. In all this is symbolized the union of Love, Energy, and the Mind of Man by whose beneficent operations all things, all forms of life, are henceforth to flourish. During the reign of Jupiter, power withdrawn for tyrannical ends and manifested in violence, in

[22] *Ibid.*, pp. 132, 185.

lightning, had left the Earth cold. From her bosom her children had drawn disease and pain. Now in the warmth of an immortal youth, with energy restored and turned to beneficent ends, the whole world will rejoice and prosper.

The Spirit of the Earth is to guide Prometheus and Asia to the "destined cave" beside which is a temple which was once dedicated to Prometheus, whose emblem was the lamp:

> . . . even as those
> Who bear the untransmitted torch of hope
> Into the grave, across the night of life,
> As thou hast borne it most triumphantly
> To this far goal of Time.

I do not see in this much that is recondite. I take it to mean simply that the Religion of Humanity is to replace the evil religions of the past, that Prometheus rather than Jupiter is to be worshiped, and that from the cave whence issued once the oracular gases which lured the nations to war, are to issue light and energy for man's service.

Scene iv

Scene 4 of Act III, with which the drama as originally conceived was to end, is largely scientific. Act IV, an afterthought, is a yet fuller exposition of Shelley's natural philosophy; in this the electrical phenomena which are set forth in the latter part of Act III are treated more at length and their place in Shelley's philosophy is more expressly defined. Scene 4 of Act III may be considered as a preliminary sketch for this scientific exposition.

It is in the work of Erasmus Darwin that is to be found the key to the Spirit of the Earth with its "light, like a green star."[23] The Spirit of the Earth is electricity, or perhaps, more precisely, atmospheric electricity. With this meaning in mind

[23] For the scientific proofs see, *ibid.,* p. 121, *et seq.*

it is not hard to see that the poetic account of its activities is a figurative rendering of the activities of atmospheric electricity as Shelley had learned of them in Erasmus Darwin and Beccaria.[24]   The green star is characteristic of the light of a copper or silver terminal of a Leyden jar.   The splendor which "drops in flakes" suggests the scintillations of the light and its phosphorescent character.   The association of electricity with the phenomena of phosphorescence I have elsewhere demonstrated.[25]

Shelley symbolically describes the Spirit of the Earth as the guide or pilot of the planet, its light shining like a crest and identifying the earth among the "populous constellations." Electricity is, too, characteristic of every drop of moisture. Therefore the light "floats along the spray of the salt sea" and likewise it "makes its chariot of a foggy cloud."[26]   When it "walks through fields or cities" and "o'er the mountaintops" it is identifiable with the will-o'-the-wisp or with the shooting stars, both, it was believed, in part electrical phenomena.[27]

"Before Jove reigned" the Spirit of the Earth "loved our sister Asia"—the spirit of Love and Beauty in Nature—and "came each leisure hour to drink the liquid light out of her eyes"—a passage descriptive of the return of atmospheric electricity to its source, the earth and sea, in its unceasing round. The dread advent of Jove has interrupted this beneficent course of nature.   The Spirit of the Earth has been separated from Asia and, as elsewhere appears, perverted to the evil purposes of Jove.   Energy, power, has been seized by Jove and used destructively as in the lightning and kindred phenomena. Now Asia can cherish the Spirit of the Earth unenvied and it can play beside her in the long noons

When work is none in the bright silent air.[28]

[24] *Ibid.*, pp. 119, 126, 127, 129.
[25] *Ibid.*, p. 133.   [26] *Ibid.*, p. 127.   [27] *Ibid.*, p. 128.   [28] *Ibid.*, p. 129.

In a long passage the Spirit of the Earth, which serves as messenger, pilot, and observer to the Earth, describes the transformation of all evil things to things beautiful and good:

> All things had put their evil nature off.

The snakes, the poisonous berries, "venomous and malicious beasts," and all the "foul masks" of men are translated. From every evil creature falls its "foul disguise," and even "toads, snakes, and efts" are beautiful. The evil and good in nature exist as the will of man is evil or good. So Shelley explicitly declares. The implications of this belief will be considered in the summary and evaluation of Shelley's philosophy.

The closer union of earth and moon, the restoration to the moon of heat and life, and a progeny of "sphered fires" to "fill the interlunar air" have their scientific implications in electricity and magnetism and the formation of meteors. These I have elsewhere discussed.[29] The general thesis is the one repeatedly touched upon that fertility, warmth, and beneficence in all material things derive from mind and love as personified in Prometheus and Asia. Love is thought of in a dual aspect, as an emotion and as an actual physical force, electricity. Thus—

> the impalpable thin air
> And the all-circling sunlight were transformed,
> As if the sense of love, dissolved in them,
> Had folded itself round the spherèd world.

Love, energy, electricity, heat are thought of as one, or as but aspects of the ether which, in Newtonian hypothesis,[30] is the source of energy, life, and matter.

To the Spirit of the Hour is given the long speech which, in Shelley's original intent, was to conclude the drama. In it may be sought the summary of Shelley's philosophy in this

[29] *Ibid.*, p. 159.　　　　[30] *Ibid.*, p. 100.

poem save as elaborated in his after-thought, the lyric fourth act. The Spirit of the Hour sees "into the mysteries of the universe" and these, while to a slight degree physical and scientific in character, are for the most part mental and social, an emphasis which one would expect in Shelley's thought. The scientific allusion occurs in the lines,

> My coursers sought their birthplace in the sun
> Where they henceforth will live exempt from toil,
> Pasturing flowers of vegetable fire.

The coursers feed on electric energy,[31] and the source of energy is the sun.

The Spirit of the Hour describes

> A temple, gazed upon by Phidian forms
> Of thee, and Asia, and the Earth, and me
> And yon fair nymphs, looking the love we feel,

the temple, presumably, to which the Earth referred in an earlier passage. The several descriptions of temples in the drama are evidence of the great impression which the ruins of Greek temples in southern Italy had made upon Shelley. The poetic descriptions are echoes of the descriptions in his letters to Peacock. The details might perhaps be traced to specific originals, the Temple of Isis for one.

The transformed human society described by the Spirit of the Hour is consistent with Shelley's oft-expressed social ideals. Indeed, a study of *Queen Mab, The Revolt of Islam,* and *Prometheus Unbound* reveals in all a Utopia which changes very little. In this respect Shelley's philosophy is consistent from first to last, but the poetic expression of it gains tremendously in power in ten years. *Queen Mab* is rhetorical though eloquent; *The Revolt of Islam* is to me tedious and somehow remote; while *Prometheus* is vigorous and compact.

---

[31] *Ibid.,* p. 131.

The gain is due in part, I suspect, to the superiority of blank verse to the Spenserian stanza and to irregular verse forms as a medium for the expression of philosophic ideas. Also in his employment of his favorite images Shelley, after much practise, attains a facility which endows them with deeper meanings and richer implications, albeit such as are increasingly difficult to define in simple prose.

The changed earth which the Spirit of the Hour depicts is, of course, kingless

> . . . and men walked
> One with the other even as spirits do—
> None frowned, none trampled; hate, disdain, or fear,
> Self-love or self-contempt on human brows
> No more inscribed, as o'er the gate of hell,
> "All hope abandon, ye who enter here."
> None fawned, none trembled, none with eager fear
> Gazed on another's eye of cold command,
> Until the subject of a tyrant's will
> Became, worse fate, the abject of his own.

Anarchism is from first to last Shelley's ideal of human society but his views as to the date and means of its attainment altered very considerably. Certainly his *Philosophic View of Reform* is a cautious, almost conservative, expression of practical political ideas. In *Prometheus Unbound* the ideal society, though an anarchy, is achieved, be it observed, only as man has attained moral perfection.

An interesting aspect of the picture drawn by the Spirit of the Hour of the old social order now destroyed, is the emphasis upon the perversion of man's nature due to it. Material and economic ills are not, in this passage, alluded to. Man is depicted as abject, as one who tramples in his heart "the sparks of love and hope"; he is "a soul self-consumed," "a vampire among men." Mistrust and hypocrisy are man's characteristic attributes in the reign of Jupiter. Shelley's picture of human society is in this reminiscent of Godwin's *Political Justice;* for though in his philosophy and metaphysics Shelley early outgrew his preceptor, in his conception of human society and the evils thereof he remains to the end a disciple.

In his feministic ideas, also, Shelley seems to me consistently Godwinian from first to last, though it should be added that not only Godwin but Mary Wollstonecraft and Lawrence contributed to his ideal of enfranchised womanhood. It is the freeing of woman from the restraints of law and custom so that she may express her love purely that Shelley emphasizes in his picture of her as she is sometime to be:

> . . . gentle radiant forms,
> From custom's evil taint exempt and pure;
> Speaking the wisdom once they could not think,
> Looking emotions once they feared to feel,
> And changed to all which once they dared not be,
> Yet being now, make earth like heaven; nor pride,
> Nor jealousy, nor envy, nor ill shame,
> The bitterest of those drops of treasured gall,
> Spoiled the sweet taste of the nepenthe, love.

Shelley's ideal is one of free love, of a virtuous promiscuity, an ideal realized, to be sure, only as man becomes regenerate and ruled by love not lust. It is from this conception that the literary critics of the Regency averted their eyes and for which, and for kindred blasphemies about religion, Shelley bore the reputation of immorality and atheism. The desertion of Harriet and the elopement with Mary Shelley, much debated as they have been, were in the eyes of the world venial sins as compared with Shelley's philosophical defense of free love. It is a paradox which forever waylays the student of social morals and forever surprises him.

The evil of man's life is, in Shelley's eyes, born of tyranny, custom, and religion. The third act concludes with a characteristic broadside against all religions and all gods—

> . . . those foul shapes, abhorred by god and man,
> Which, under many a name and many a form
> Strange, savage, ghastly, dark, and execrable,
> Were Jupiter, the tyrant of the world.

In the Promethean day their shrines are tenantless. The "dark yet mighty faith" which was "a power as wide as is the world it wasted" is presumably Christianity, though it matters not what, for in Shelley's belief all institutional religion was inevitably tyrannical and evil; all, in Voltaire's words, infamous. Innumerable passages could be cited from Voltaire, Godwin, and Holbach of which Shelley's words are the echo. I cannot see that as regards institutional religion Shelley's beliefs in *Prometheus* are any different from those expressed in *Queen Mab,* though his conception of Christ is completely altered in the later poem.

Again in the last lines is repeated the image of life as a veil:

> The painted veil, by those who were, called life
> Which mimicked, as with colors idly spread,
> All men believed or hoped, is torn aside.

The meaning, I suppose, is that the character of actuality, the product of man's thought, is wholly altered. It was a "loathsome mask" and when torn aside reality is unveiled. The actuality of earthly life now conforms to the real existence which formerly lay, concealed, behind. In this reality man is

> Sceptreless, free, uncircumscribed, but man
> Equal, unclassed, tribeless, and nationless,
> Exempt from awe, worship, degree, the king
> Over himself.

This is the anarchy of Shelley's ideal.

Yet it is important to note and to weigh in an evaluation of Shelley's philosophy that man's earthly heaven is not the heaven of the Buddhistic or Platonic philosophers. Man's enfranchised life is not one of contemplation, Nirvana, absorption in the infinite. It is the best and most intense realization of earthly possibilities. Man is

> . . . just, gentle, wise: but man
> Passionless?—no, yet free from guilt or pain,
> Which were, for his will made or suffered them. . . .

Nor is man

> . . . yet exempt, though ruling them like slaves,
> From chance and death, and mutability,
> The clogs of that which else might oversoar
> The loftiest star of unascended heaven,
> Pinnacled dim in the intense inane.

The interpretation of these lines has been in part anticipated in earlier passages of this commentary, and more will be said of them in the concluding evaluation of Shelley's philosophy. Meanwhile there is the fourth act yet to be weighed, with whatever new contribution it may make to Shelley's thought, or refinements it may suggest upon ideas already advanced.

PROMETHEUS UNBOUND: ACT IV

"SHELLEY develops, more particularly in the lyrics of this drama, his abstruse and imaginative theories with regard to the Creation." If these, Mrs. Shelley's words, are just, we should look to the lyrical fourth act of *Prometheus Unbound* for much of Shelley's most recondite thought. The fourth act is a philosophical epilogue in which Shelley does two things: he depicts the joy of the liberated world, and he sets forth symbolically his theories of mind and matter. The metaphysics and natural philosophy incidental to the first three acts are here the entire theme and are blent to what is, in effect, a reconciliation of neo-Platonism with the scientific speculation of Shelley's day. It is extraordinary that he should have put thoughts so abstract and so abstruse into the form of lyrics. Yet his symbolical habit of mind enabled him to do so successfully. The difficulty for the interpreter lies not in the form but in the interpretation of the symbols employed.

I have elsewhere explained the purely scientific allusions of the fourth act, have argued the difficult passages, and supported my contentions with parallel passages from the scientific writings of Shelley's day.[1] It will suffice in the ensuing discussion to repeat these findings without arguing them. More important it is to reconcile them with neo-Platonism or whatever other philosophy we shall discover. The fourth act should, presumably, if rightly interpreted, reinforce the findings in the three previous acts. For it is a justifiable assumption that Shelley's philosophy is, as a whole, consistent; that in the interval between the conclusion of the third act and the writing of the fourth, it did not greatly alter; but that in the fourth act, his purpose being more singly philosophical, ideas handled with some poetic freedom in the earlier acts, or

[1] *A Newton Among Poets.*

[125]

even, perhaps, not wholly thought through, are here more fully and consistently set forth.

The initial lyric of the Unseen Spirits plunges at once into metaphysics. The dark forms are "spectres of the dead Hours" which "bear Time to his tomb in eternity." The imagery of the hours is perhaps derived from Proclus (Taylor),

> Heaven's sounding gates kept by the winged hours

being symbolic of terrene life, which exists in time, the "envious shadow" cast by the throne of Saturn. The new day of Prometheus is, therefore, by implication, timeless, and in this respect identical with the timeless universe which exists in the mind of the One. I have before remarked that I am unable to grasp this conception as true of a living world, for thought itself is sequential and therefore creates time. Yet the idea is common to neo-Platonism and other philosophies, whence, presumably, Shelley derived it.

The "past Hours" flee

> To the dark, to the past, to the dead,

bearing with them

> . . . . the spoil which their toil
> Raked together
> From the conquest but One could foil.

Who is the One? The problem was encountered at the very outset of our study in the second line of the poem

> Monarch of Gods and Daemons, and all Spirits
> But One . . .

Is the One Prometheus, or is it that Eternal Love mentioned by Demogorgon as the sole power superior to "Fate, Time, Occasion, Chance, and Change?" Or again, does the One become incarnate in Prometheus? Is Eternal Love so made manifest? More plausibly, perhaps, is Prometheus the incar-

nation of the second, the intellectual hypostasis of the One?
Perhaps further study of the fourth act will support some one
of these surmises. It is sufficient for the moment to think of
the One as the ultimate and eternal God who, existing above
time, foils the conquest of the hours.

The Voice of Unseen Spirits summons a Semi-chorus of
Hours who refer to the Unseen Spirits as the "Spirits of Air
and Earth." We encounter soon, also, the Spirits of the Human Mind. Earth, Air, and Mind—matter, heaven, and being—are thus symbolized and their union celebrated. There
is in this symbolism no inherent difficulty of interpretation,
though the machinery is tenuous and insubstantial after Shelley's characteristic manner. But I find it not easy to explain
the reappearance of the Hours, for Time has been but lately
borne "to his tomb in eternity." It does not wholly satisfy to
declare that the "dark forms and shadows" which previously
appeared are the ghosts of the past and that the past is thus
ceremoniously interred. Not only the past but Time itself had
supposedly been disposed of.

The Semichorus of Hours whose appearance is thus discon-
certing involve us in fresh perplexities in their explanation of
their origin. That the Spirits of Air and Earth have

> . . . . drawn back the figured curtain of sleep
> Which covered our being and darkened our birth
> In the deep

is, I assume, a statement that the future is to be revealed by
the Spirits of Air and Earth, and that these personify Power,
for Semichorus I, presumably of the Hours, a few lines later
declare:

> We have heard the lute of Hope in sleep;
>   We have known the voice of Love in dreams;
> We have felt the wand of Power, and leap—

The Hours of the future, then, are awaked by Power from their sleep of "an hundred ages." So far so good. The Hours of the past which had been

> Cradled in visions of hate and care

had each upon awakening

> Found the truth—
> Worse than his visions were.

Whereas the unawakened hours had "heard the lute of Hope in sleep," had dreamt of Love, and had finally been awakened by the "wand of Power." These last, these happier Hours, are those which celebrate the Promethean Day.

But what of the origin of these Hours whose birth is "in the deep" or, as the second Semichorus replies, "below the deep"? Shelley's philosophic meaning I take to be that the birth of the hours—the origin of time—is beyond the deep of the material universe, and is to be found in the mysterious source of all things, the One. From Saturn "Time fell, an envious shadow." This is as intelligible as most metaphysical speculations upon the nature of time and eternity. But how then explain the appearance of the hours in what is, presumably, a timeless universe? Consistency is here perhaps to be extorted through the fact that all the future Hours come to life at once. The whole of futurity is thus manifest in the present instant. This interpretation is supported by the line

> And each who waked as his brother slept.

In the past the hours waked singly to the miseries of earthly being. Now all are awakened to sing as a chorus the delights of a happier day. Time thenceforth ceases to be.

Yet it is not certain that Shelley remains true to this conception of a timeless Promethean universe. In his later picture of the activities of liberated humanity, their creative enterprises and their invention and practise of new arts, he premises time. Necessarily, for a dynamic state of being, he must do so. The metaphysical conception of a timeless universe is incompatible with the idea of an evolving universe. Nor is there the possibility in a timeless universe of an end. Yet Shelley in depicting the Promethean day speculates upon the chance of its destruction and reconstruction. Either or both are possible only in Time. The philosophy of the poem here confronts an inevitable paradox, one of the antinomies of Kant. Seemingly it is one insoluble to the human reason.

The Chorus of Hours sings:

> Once the hungry Hours were hounds
> Which chased the day like a bleeding deer . . .

Now in a happier day

> Let the Hours, and the Spirits of might and pleasure
> Like the clouds and sunbeams, unite.

Time, energy, and pleasure become one in the day of mankind's liberation. The union is expressed in one of Shelley's favorite figures, the drawing by the sun of water-vapor to form the cloud, symbol of endless change, endless unity, in the round of generation. And to the spirits of might and pleasure, at one now in a timeless universe—eternally wedded—are joined also the Spirits of the Human Mind, symbolizing the eternal joy of liberated mankind in the exercise of its newly-found powers.

The chorus of the Spirits of the Human Mind is replete with Shelleyan symbolism. The place whence they come was once "so dusk, and obscene, and blind," but

> Now 'tis an ocean
> Of clear emotion,
> A heaven of serene and mighty motion.

The idea is one already familiar. From the ocean of being, symbol of unity, we have seen that the individual soul is separated and to it at last returns. In the Promethean day the stress is no longer upon the individual minds but upon the oneness of all minds: a unity of emotion as well as of thought, and though forever in motion, serene. The effectiveness of the recurrent symbol is, in this instance, particularly notable.

Of the two neo-Platonic images employed in the second stanza of the song, one is already familiar. The Spirits of the Mind come

> From that deep abyss
> Of wonder and bliss,
> Whose caverns are crystal palaces;

The implication is that in the new age the caverns of individual thought are lucent, that every mind is open to the light of all other minds. Yet the individuality of mind is also stressed. This is again a metaphor which symbolizes multiplicity in unity.

The last three lines of the stanza introduce a new symbol:

> From those skyey towers
> Where Thought's crowned powers
> Sit watching your dance, ye happy Hours.

The towers here symbolize the outward looking aspects of the mind; they are the seat of the thought which is based upon observation as distinguished from the introspective thought characteristic of the cave. Broadly interpreted, towers are symbols of scientific thought and artistic creation, whereas caverns are symbolic of philosophic meditation. Tower, in Shelley's employment of the word, sometimes means isolation or detachment—

> Apart from men, as in a lonely tower
> —*Prince Athanase*, l. 33.

Whence is derivable the idea of wisdom, the product of detached observation of life

> . . . yet not alone from wisdom's tower.
> —*The Revolt of Islam,* II, xx, 8.

Succeeding stanzas of the Chorus of Spirits repeat the symbolism of the inward and outward way of thought and emotion. Love is conceived of as secret, egocentric:

> From the dim recesses
> Of woven caresses
> Where lovers catch ye by your loose tresses. . . .

Wisdom again, likened previously to a tower, is thus characterized:

> From the azure isles
> Where sweet Wisdom smiles
> Delaying your ships with her siren wiles.

The lines are addressed to the Hours, who it is, as though borne in ships, are delayed at the isles of Wisdom, the Circe who lures them with her wiles. I gather from this, simply, that the charms of knowledge, as of love, so beguile men from the sense of time that in their absorption in knowledge, time ceases to be. Love and wisdom are the preoccupations of a world no longer heedful of time.

The next stanza repeats the dual aspect of the mental life:

> From the temples high
> Of man's ear and eye
> Roofed over Sculpture and Poesy.

Like the towers of thought and wisdom the temples of ear and eye are outward looking, dealing with sensations necessarily derived from without but which are turned to the inward creation of Sculpture and Poesy. The inner and outer powers here work in unison. Likewise in the pursuit of science,

though the emphasis is on the outer universe, the inner inspiration is symbolized by the figure "springs," employed
constantly by Shelley with the implication of inspiration or
intuition:

> From the murmurings
> Of the unsealed springs
> Where Science bedews her Daedal wings.

The imagery, though at first sight seemingly remote and
strained, is, upon study and the citation of parallels, intelligible
and consistent enough. Shelley could not have realized how
difficult to one unfamiliar with his thought processes, his
habitual imagery might seem.

The two concluding stanzas of the lyric, though highly
metaphorical, present no particular difficulties. "Islets" is employed as isles previously, symbolical of a place of rest, of
security, in the restless sea of experience—

> And the islets were few
> Where the bud-blighted flowers of happiness grew.

"Dew," one of the most frequent of Shelley's symbols, is employed characteristically—

> And the dew of our wings is a rain of balm.

Dew is one of the congruent group of images which depict
the round of existence—cloud, stream, fountain, etc. It is employed with the connotations of gentleness, healing, and divine
origin, as in the following instances:

> If nursed by the selectest dew of love
> > —*The Cenci,* IV, i, 123.
>
> If sleep, that healing dew of heaven
> > —*The Cenci,* IV, i, 178.
>
> . . . and the dew of music more divine
> > —*Ginevra,* l. 115.

A dew rained down by God above
                    —*Peter,* V, iv, 5.

Fall like a dew of balm upon the world.
                    —*Q. Mab,* VI, 53.

The Spirits and the Hours join in a chorus:

> Then weave the web of the mystic measure;
>   From the depths of the sky and the ends of the earth,
> Come, swift Spirits of might and pleasure,
>   Fill the dance and the music of mirth,—
> As the waves of a thousand streams rush by
> To an ocean of splendour and harmony!

The union of might and pleasure repeats an idea previously expressed and the conclusion employs the familiar symbols of stream and ocean. Stream symbolizes the individual life, ocean the sum of being. Multiplicity in unity is again the theme.

The ensuing chorus, that of the Spirits of the Mind rejoicing in their liberation, prophesies their creative activity. They sing:

> We are free to dive, or soar, or run;
>   Beyond or around,
>   Or within the bound
> Which clips the earth with darkness round.

They will pass "into the hoar deep" beyond the stars, there to dispel "Death, Chaos, and Night." From their singing shall be built

> In the void's loose field
> A world for the Spirit of Wisdom to wield.

The more technical astronomical allusions in these stanzas I have elsewhere discussed and need not now dwell upon.[2] The larger implications are not difficult. The liberated mind

[2] *Ibid.,* chap. X.

of man becomes the creator of its own universe, bringing love
and unity from discord and anarchy. And as the mind so
creates,

> . . . Love, Thought, and Breath
> The powers that quell Death,
> Wherever we soar shall assemble beneath.

With these spiritual or immaterial realities is associated

> . . . the Spirit of Might,
> Which drives round the stars in their fiery flight . . .

This association of Love, Energy, Thought, and Life we
have already encountered. "Love which is as fire" is, in Shelley's symbolism, electricity. And Life as identified both with
Love and electricity is so defined in various passages as

> . . . I wandered once
> With Asia, drinking life from her loved eyes.
> —I, 122-23.

And again, Love,

> That planet-crested Shape swept by on lightning-braided pinions,
>   Scattering the liquid joy of life from his ambrosial tresses:
> His footsteps paved the world with light. . . .
> —I, 763-68.

That all forms of energy—light, electricity, magnetism, and
the force of gravitation—were but functions of the "electric
ether" was an hypothesis of Newton's which, with subsequent
scientific theory of a similar tenor, I need not here recapit-
ulate.[3] The congruity of this theory with neo-Platonic speculation should be evident. In Platonism and neo-Platonism
thought and the spirit of life are the ultimate realities. The
One in his triune nature is the mysterious source of all—
thought, energy, life. His thought creates the designs which
the creative energy materializes in the objective world. If the

---

[3] *Ibid.*, p. 100.

mysterious energy which makes possible this creation be
thought of in neo-Platonic terms, as life or love and in the
Newtonian concept as the ether emanating from God, the
similarity of the mystical philosophy to the scientific theory
is manifestly close. In Shelley's philosophy the two—mysticism of neo-Platonic origin, and Newtonian scientific theory
—are fused.

Order is to be brought out of chaos by the Spirits of Mind.
A world is to be created for "the Spirit of Wisdom to wield."
Man is to design his own universe. Not only does he find
heaven on earth, a place of love and aesthetic satisfactions, but
he reaches out to create endlessly new worlds for the dominion
of joy and wisdom. Man it is clear has usurped the powers of
divinity, has grown into God, identifiable henceforth, I believe
Shelley means to imply, with the intellectual, or second hypostasis of the One. But of this profound conception I shall
have more to say in my concluding comment on Shelley's
philosophy.

The semichoruses of spirits display their contrasted functions: some are creative forces organizing a new universe from
Chaos; others control the universe already under the reign of
law. Some preside at the birth of a new world as it evolves
and becomes a "gathering sphere"[4] and

> . . . the trees, and the beasts, and the clouds appear
> From its chaos made calm by love, not fear.

Clouds are the symbol of generation and the round of human
existence. And again, love is the synonym for ordered power,
for constructive energy.

In the concluding chorus symbols now familiar reappear:

> Break the dance, and scatter the song
> Let some depart, and some remain;

[4] *Ibid.*, p. 166.

Wherever we fly we lead along
In leashes, like star-beams, soft yet strong,
    The clouds that are heavy with love's sweet rain.

The cloud, symbol of fertility and life, bears "love's sweet rain," the "electric rains" without which there can be no verdure, no life. The clouds are led "in leashes like star-beams," guided that is, by invisible electric force. The cloud, thus, in its formation and in its function is guided and animated by an energy which is electricity or "love," as you choose to define it. To Shelley the terms "material" and "immaterial" were of little meaning.[5] He conceived of energy as a spiritual force, as love, when benificently employed, and as hate if devoted to evil purposes. In the symbol of the cloud he suggests the identification of love with energy in creating and fostering life. And as the cloud symbolizes also the round of creation, the life cycle of the elements, and, similarly, the life cycle of individual souls, the frequency with which the symbol is employed by Shelley and its all-important place in his mythology is accounted for.

The spirits vanish, whereupon Ione speaks of "new notes," an "awful sound" now audible, and Panthea replies that it is "the deep music of the rolling world." The pauses of the world's "aeolian modulations" are filled with "under-notes"—

    Clear, silver, icy, keen awakening tones.

As the ensuing apparitions are symbolical of earth and moon, these "keen awakening tones," the "under-notes," presumably are those of the moon. The descriptive stress is upon the coldness and brightness, appropriate attributes which are strengthened in the description of the child which sits within

    . . . a chariot like that thinnest boat
    In which the mother of the months is borne . . .

[5] "Eusebus and Theosophus (A Refutation of Deism)," *Prose Works of Shelley* (ed. by Forman), II, 69.

for the countenance of the child is white like snow and

Its plumes are as feathers of sunny frost.

I have elsewhere argued the scientific implications of the orb-like chariot in which the Moon-Spirit is conveyed and of the crystal sphere in which the Spirit of the Earth is laid asleep.[6] I wish now to stress rather the general philosophic implications of these readings. These I believe to be in harmony with what we have already found in earlier passages of the poem. And the symbols likewise, as I interpret them, are neo-Platonic in character and congruous with the scientific imagery.

The chariot and the sphere which symbolize moon and earth make their appearance "through two openings in the forest" preluded by the "aeolian modulations" and the "keen awakening tones." The association of music with these apparitions recalls an earlier and kindred use in the light of which the moon and earth passage is intelligible. The souls driven to incarnation, it will be recalled, think that they obey their own "sweet desires" but are in reality obedient to the "storm of sound."

> There those enchanted eddies play
> Of echoes, music-tongued, which draw,
> By Demogorgon's mighty law,
> With melting rapture, or sweet awe,
> All spirits on that secret way,
> As inland boats are driven to Ocean
> Down streams made strong with mountain-thaw.
> —II, scene 2, ll. 41-47.

The use of music as an impelling force was reminiscent, it was observed, of Rosicrucian theory.[7]

There are notable parallels between the imagery of this

---

[6] *A Newton Among Poets*, p. 140 *et seq.*
[7] See p. 90, *supra.*

passage and that descriptive of the apparitions of the child spirits. The "two visions of strange radiance" appear through "two openings in the forest" from which emerge "two runnels of a rivulet" whose path is melody. The visions float "Upon the ocean-like enchantment of strong sound," sound which flows

> Under the ground and through the windless air.

The familiar stream and ocean motif is evidently symbolic of the round of generation: separation from the ocean of universal being and return thereto; but the terms of the image are either in the metaphor of music rather than water; or, it may be meant, the generative round is impelled by and accompanied by music. In either case Shelley evidently is describing some phase of creation whose law is musical, and which is obedient to some rhythm.

As is shortly manifest, the description is of the spirits of earth and moon, who appear as infants, a conception which is the more intelligible when it is recalled that in the Platonic and neo-Platonic philosophy, earth, moon, and planets are thought to be endowed with personalities, are indeed gods. Earth and moon in Shelley's conception are experiencing a new birth in the Promethean day and the description of the child spirits is symbolic of this rejuvenescence. In it are symbolically depicted their powers and characteristics—the nature, that is to say, of matter in its earthly and lunar manifestations.

That this is a just interpretation is clear from the subsequent portrayal of natural forces of earth and moon and from a due consideration of the initial phrase "through two openings in the forest." The "forest" in neo-Platonic imagery is symbolic of matter[8] and was in this sense employed in the description of the journey of Asia and Panthea to Demogorgon. Of Demogorgon they ask answers to the riddle of life.

[8] See p. 60, *supra*.

They journey, therefore, to the preëxistent state, to the reality that lies beneath material things and beyond the illusions of sense. So, in the later instance, analogously, Shelley means, I think, to imply in the "two openings in the forest" revelations of the true, the occult, character of the natural forces manifest in the earth and moon. The ensuing passages embody his scientific concepts of these forces.

Ione's description is of the symbols which depict the nature of the moon. The scientific character of this picture I have elsewhere discussed[9] and need here but briefly summarize. The "winged infant" whose "plumes are as feathers of sunny frost" metaphorically describes the moon with its white un-refracted light, its cold, and its lack of atmosphere. The "liquid darkness" is the heat which, because of the moon's lack of atmosphere, radiates in the dark heat rays,[10] the "fire that is not brightness." Also it is implied that the moon is one pole of an electric circuit of which the earth is the other; the characteristic emanation of the moon being white light "scat-tered in strings," descriptive of the brush of the positive pole, as the star is descriptive of the colorful negative pole.[11]

From the second opening of the wood rushes the sphere in which lies a child, the Spirit of the Earth, asleep. In the de-scription of the sphere "which is as many thousand spheres" is embodied Shelley's conception of the nature of matter,[12] a conception involving the speculations of Newton and Davy in which matter and force are identical, are both electric. Espe-cially is Shelley's imagery in accord with the electrical theory of matter advanced by Davy.[13] The "orbs involving and in-volved" are reminiscent of passages in Erasmus Darwin, whose theory of matter and force, in the Newtonian tradition, is similar to Davy's.[14]

[9] *A Newton Among Poets*, p. 151 *et seq.*   [10] *Ibid.*
[11] *Ibid.*, p. 155.   [12] *Ibid.*, p. 141.   [13] *Ibid.*, p. 142.   [14] *Ibid.*, p. 141.

But mixed with this advanced scientific speculation, so curiously and so accurately set forth in sensuous images, is a philosophy of another origin. The "unimaginable shapes" which inhabit this dance of matter is a phrase reminiscent of the gnomes and sylphs of Rosicrucian lore. The best gloss upon the passage which I have found is in Paracelsus, who describes the characteristics of these elemental beings. The poetic value of such symbols to personify the forms of matter is evident, and they have been employed by numerous poets including Erasmus Darwin in the scientific epics to which Shelley is so curiously indebted. But beneath the convenient imagery lies, in Shelley's employment, a belief in the living quality of matter; to this faith Shelley explicitly commits himself not only in this instance but in others. Even in *Queen Mab,* Shelley, despite his youthful belief in determinism, had early declared that all matter, to the most minute atom, was alive.

Such a faith has a philosophical lineage. A distinction was early made between matter—inert and lifeless—and mind—moving and alive. But with the progress of science it was surmised that matter, though seemingly inert, was not really so. The elements might spin "upon a thousand sightless axles" and in the balance of their interplay produce the illusion of complete rest. Self-determined motion, thereupon, ceased to be a distinguishing test of matter and mind. In this respect matter and mind were the same. The inference might be that all was matter, that mind did not exist save as a function of matter, or that all was mind and that matter did not exist. Shelley in his maturer thought refused to quarrel over the terms.[15] Whether you called all spirit matter or all matter spirit was of no importance to him. But he was firm in the conviction that all which was seemingly inert was in reality

[15] See p. 100, note 5 *supra.*

alive in the common and usual meaning of the word; the entire universe and every atom in it was alive, the home of an invisible being, an animated presence—gods of earth, moon, and sun; gnomes of the earth, and the sylphs of the air. The nomenclature of these beings was borrowed from the neo-Platonic and Rosicrucian philosophies and was a poetic convenience in symbolical expression.

Various and otherwise divergent philosophies lend support to this belief in animated matter. That Shelley accepted it for poetic purposes is evident. That he more profoundly believed it as an article of religious faith is, I think, also true. He expresses the conviction both in prose and verse, early and late, even though, as in *Queen Mab,* it is difficult to reconcile his belief with the scientific materialism which he then professed. It is a form of pantheism, kin to the vague pantheism of Wordsworth with its immanent deity; and to the pantheism of Spinoza to whom the visible universe is the garment of God. Yet it is precisely neither of these.

The note of Shelley's pantheism, if it can accurately be called such, or better, perhaps, his immaterialism, his belief that all matter is spirit, is multiplicity rather than unity. That the manifold forms of life are embraced in a larger unity he accepts in theory, but the poetic emphasis is certainly upon the individual constituent part—cloud, sky-lark, west wind. In Wordsworth the individual flower is the clue to the immanent deity, evidence of his all-pervading presence; whereas in Shelley there is delight in the thing in itself as possessed of its own character and free will. It is an emphasis consonant with Erasmus Darwin's belief in the evolutionary growth of life through individual adaptation into richer and more varied forms. It is in accord, too, with Shelley's extreme individualism, his belief in anarchism as a social program. Multiplicity in unity is the essence of Shelley's belief, but his concern as a poet is more with the enrichment of life through the multi-plication and improvement of the individual forms than their return to unity in Nirvana. Life-weary he sometimes cries out in homesickness, but the mood is transient. He is not so much weary of life in itself as of human life as it now is, so remote from his dream of what earthly life might become.

In his symbolic description of elemental forces Shelley remains constant to his electrical theory of matter, a theory deriving from Newton and Davy.[16] The star upon the forehead of the Spirit of the Earth is the star of the negative electrode, gold and azure; and the spears of light are reminiscent of the aurora borealis.[17] The tyrant-quelling myrtle, whether symbolic only of peaceful victory or whether usurping the powers of the laurel as a charm against lightning, implies energy devoted to the works of love rather than those of hate.[18] The sunlike lightnings are the electrical energy generated by the earth in its rotation and given off in the aurora.[19] These lightnings "pierce the dark soil" and reveal earth's secrets, implying as I have elsewhere demonstrated either the discovery of new elements by the electro-chemical methods of analysis perfected by Davy,[20] or a phenomenon similar to the X-ray.

Recondite as this symbolism may at first sight seem it is remarkably consistent, and once the reader becomes habituated to it and is at home in Shelley's mental processes, it is no longer incredible nor particularly difficult. That Shelley must not be held to minute fidelity to proved scientific fact in his depiction of natural phenomena and the uses to which electricity may be put in the disclosure of hidden things will I think be conceded. He is, after all, giving an imaginative, a poetical vision of the tools which the emancipated mind will have at its disposal in the mastery and understanding of nat-

---

[16] *A Newton Among Poets*, chaps. VI-VII.
[17] *Ibid.*, p. 145.   [18] *Ibid.*, p. 149.   [19] *Ibid.*, p. 147.   [20] *Ibid.*, p. 148.

ural forces. Electrical energy is to reveal the nature of the elements, "to pierce the dark soil." The means here I take to be the methods of Davy, electro-chemical analysis. But the "sun-like lightnings" also reveal the "secrets of the earth's deep heart" in a less metaphorical and more literal sense. The X-ray of much later discovery would seem best adapted to this purpose. That Shelley had encountered any theoretical anticipation of such an agent I have nowhere found, but such an anticipation is not impossible. The scientific literature of his age is vast, speculative, and often prophetic in its hypotheses. Certainly it was universally understood that the most solid matter is porous. Shelley himself in several instances employs the word "pore" quite in its scientific meaning. If the electricity generated within the earth[21] were luminous in its emanation, it would reveal the secrets of the earth's interior, acting like the X-ray of modern discovery. Shelley may mean in his lines either this, or the use of electro-chemical analysis to discover the elements of matter. Perhaps he implies both meanings.

Through the "sun-like lightnings," then, the literal deeps of the earth no less than the secrets of its elements, are to be revealed; and in the ensuing long description Shelley depicts his conception of the earth's interior, its geology, and of ancient civilizations and forms of prehistoric life buried within it. He had scientific sources for these details, sources which evidently intrigued his imagination.[22] There is clear evidence that he subscribed also to the evolutionary theory of man's ascent from lower forms of life, a theory with which he was familiar in the works of Erasmus Darwin and presumably others—Helvetius and Diderot perhaps. The passage,

> The wrecks beside of many a city vast,
> Whose population which the earth grew over
> Was mortal, but not human . . .

[21] *Ibid.* [22] *Ibid.*, p. 176.

implies either a non-human ancestor for mankind or prehistoric races destroyed by a tidal wave or other cataclysm.[23]

There are also lines descriptive of prehistoric life as revealed by the paleontologist.[24]

> The jagged alligator, and the might
> Of earth-convulsing behemoth, which once
> Were monarch beasts, and on the slimy shores
> And weed-overgrown continents of earth,
> Increased and multiplied like summer worms
> On an abandoned corpse, till the blue globe
> Wrapped deluge round it like a cloak, and they
> Yelled, gasped, and were abolished, or some God
> Whose throne was in a comet, passed, and cried,
> "Be not!" and like my words they were no more.

In this, Shelley subscribes to the theory of a deluge due to the passing of a comet, a theory widely held in the eighteenth century and mentioned by Davy.[25]

The antiphonal lyrics which follow the long description of prehistoric life depict the new golden age, the rejuvenescence of Earth and Moon. The Earth sings:

> The joy, the triumph, the delight, the madness!
> The boundless, overflowing, bursting gladness,
> The vaporous exultation not to be confined.

The last line is, as Mr. A. N. Whitehead has noted, no more than a "poetic transcript of 'the expansive force of gases.'"[26] The earth is resuming its youth, radiating more heat, as in the day of the supposititious golden age when the climate was uniformly mild from pole to pole.[27] This more ardent life is possible because the energy diverted by Jupiter for his evil purposes is now employed in the creative round of nature.

---

[23] *Ibid.*, p. 180.   [24] *Ibid.*, p. 175.   [25] *Ibid.*

[26] *Science and the Modern World* (New York, The Macmillan Company, 1925), p. 119.

[27] *A Newton Among Poets*, p. 26.

The Moon feels this heightened energy manifest as heat, electricity, or magnetic attraction.[28]

> Some Spirit is darted like a beam from thee
> Which penetrates my frozen frame
> And passes with the warmth of flame,
> With love, and odor, and deep melody
> Through me, through me!

All the constituents of the Earth exult as does the Moon in their strength, freed as they now are from the

> . . . Sceptred curse
> Who all our green and azure universe
> Threatenedst to muffle round with black destruction, sending
> A solid cloud to rain hot thunderstones,
> And splinter and knead down my children's bones,
> All I bring forth, to one void mass battering and blending . . .

The passage is reminiscent of the evidences of volcanic destruction such as Shelley had seen at Pompeii in 1818 and which he describes in his letters. I have elsewhere shown that electrical phenomena were believed in the science of Shelley's day to accompany volcanic action. The fact has significance in Shelley's symbolism, for it is Jupiter the usurper and tyrant who seeks in his misuse of power to destroy mankind. Electrical energy is diverted from its proper, its peaceful uses, to this end, and only as Prometheus is victorious over his foe do the disasters to which the race has been subject cease.

The catastrophes visible in the shadow of Vesuvius, and the grotto of the dogs with its poisonous gases, made a deep impression on Shelley, as his letters witness. Few evidences of the malice or indifference of nature to the lot of man are so striking, so dramatic. How is evil thus manifest to be reconciled with belief in an omnipotent, if beneficent, Providence? Either God is not synonymous with good or he is not om-

[28] *Ibid.*, p. 160.

nipotent. It is to the latter alternative that Shelley apparently
inclines. The omnipotence of God as good is evidently at best
no more than potential. The liberation of Prometheus marks
its triumph. With the Titan's conquest over himself, with his
attainment of perfect love and forgiveness, the "material"
forces of nature likewise are transformed to good. Does Shelley imply that this transformation is sympathetic, mystical?
Or that human reason, manifested in applied science, effects
it? The questions are more easily asked than answered. A
concluding evaluation of Shelley's philosophy must needs consider them.

In the transformation of the moon the phenomena are such
as would accompany the revival of internal heat. The snow
and ice melt.[29]   And with returning warmth the moon re-
covers her atmosphere; vegetation and animal life are once
more possible. The symbol of the new round of existence, of
fertility and generation, is, as usual, the cloud:

> Wingèd clouds soar here and there,
> Dark with the rain new buds are dreaming of:
> 'Tis love, all love!

Again we have the association of love with force and life, or
the identification of them as three aspects of one and the same
divine energy.

The reanimation of the Moon is synchronous with the
reanimation of the Earth. Even "in the forgotten dead" life
is reawakened:

> They breathe a spirit up from their obscurest bowers.

What precisely Shelley means in this, save as he implies that
death is not a reality in the sense that it is impermanent, I do
not know. The Platonic implications of the line,

> Death is the veil which those who live call life

[29] *Ibid.*, p. 161.

were previously noted, and lines later written, as in the *Sensitive Plant* (1820), are of similar tenor:

> It is a modest creed, and yet
> Pleasant, if one considers it,
> To own that death itself must be,
> Like all the rest, a mockery.
> —III, ll. 126-29.

Platonic, or neo-Platonic, also are

> . . . the lampless caves of unimagined being

whence has arisen like a storm or whirlwind that which shakes "thought's stagnant chaos," and hate, fear, and pain are dispelled from man. The familiar cave, symbolic of the occult ways of thought, I take here to imply the One, the mysterious source of all. A divine impulse, a divine thought, like creative light broods on the chaos of man's mind. It is another expression of the idea that as man's mind is altered, the visible material universe reflects the changes in his thought.

Man as he has been is likened to "a many-sided mirror" which distorted "to many a shape of error"

> This true fair world of things, a sea reflecting love.

The material universe, then, is but the reflection of divine love, which, however, man has distorted through the defects of his own mind. "The true fair world of things" becomes so to his sight only as he perceives reality rather than illusion. The hate and fear and pain that were existed in his own mind, not in the world without nor in the love which created it. The figure becomes more intelligible and consistent, I think, if the "many-sided mirror" is taken to be the waves upon the ocean of being, and the distortions as due to the separateness of the individual from his kind. That this is the meaning is suggested by a later line. Love is

> . . . as the sun's heaven
> Gliding o'er ocean, smooth, serene, and even.

The emphasis here is upon the unity of man in his enfranchised state, as contrasted with the separateness and disharmony of men prior thereto.

The same idea is repeated in a subsequent stanza:

> Man, oh, not men! a chain of linkèd thought
> Of love and might to be divided not.

The metaphor of the chain to suggest unity in multiplicity is analogous to that of the sea with its waves. And again we encounter the familiar conjunction of love, thought, and might which in man, as in God, is both trinity and unity, three aspects of the One: the Trinity which Plotinus graphically depicts as the two concentric circles whose ineffable center (truth, love, beauty) is portrayed as a point; the inner circle (or second hypostasis) is thought; the outer circle is the impulse to creation (energy). The whole forms the divine Triad which is the One. Does man, then, become in Shelley's figure, God? Or, made in the pattern of God, are his powers likewise triune?

Whether himself God, or created in the image of God, man as "one harmonious soul of many a soul," as a unity in multiplicity, henceforth rules matter, "the elements,"

> As the sun rules even with a tyrant's gaze
> The unquiet republic of the maze
> Of planets, struggling fierce towards heaven's free wilderness.

Man's mastery of his physical universe is like the sun's mastery of the planets. Again force and thought are defined as aspects of the One. Love rules man's will as a "tempest-wingèd ship" is guided by its helm, for man's will has subordinated "all mean passions, bad delights." Love now forces

> . . . life's wildest shores to own its sovereign sway.

The activities of man's thought when governed by love are artistic and scientific.

> . . . Through the cold mass
> Of marble and of color his dreams pass—
> Bright threads whence mothers weave the robes their children
> wear.

I take this to mean that through art the child is prenatally influenced. The figure is more intelligible in the light of the following neo-Platonic excerpt:

And what symbol is more proper to souls descending into generation, and the tenacious vestment of body, than as the poet says, "Nymphs weaving on stony beams purple garments wonderful to behold?" For the flesh is generated in and about the bones, which in the bodies of animals may be compared to stones. On which account these textorial instruments, are fashioned from stones alone. But the purple garments plainly appear to be the flesh with which we are invested. . . .[30]

In the day of man's liberation, language rules "thoughts and forms which else senseless and shapeless were," the idea previously expressed in the words "speech created thought." This notion Shelley derived, it may be, from Lord Monboddo, whose work on the origin of language is listed in Shelley's readings. The citation which I have selected is from Monboddo's *Ancient Metaphysics,* a work which Shelley may likewise have read and which in its emphasis upon and sympathy with Platonism I surmise may have supplemented Berkeley in shaping the growth of Shelley's thought.

This world of ideas, upon which I have enlarged so much, and which may be called the intellectual world of our microcosm, could never have been formed without the use of language. For, in the first place, we must have had certain signs or marks of our ideas, which would be absolutely necessary for our own use, as without them we could not retain them in our memories, or put

[30] Taylor, *Proclus,* II, 284.

them together in propositions. And, secondly, we could not otherwise have communicated them to one another. Now it is by communication, in the way of discourse, that all arts and sciences have
been invented and cultivated, and regular forms of government
framed, under which men might live in peace and good order, and
be supplied with all the necessaries of life, so that they might have
time to apply to arts and sciences. Languages, therefore, may be
said to be the parent of all arts and sciences, and to be the first
step of that ladder, by which we are to ascend from this earth to
that state from which we are fallen.[31]

In his new world, man, now wholly emancipated and free
to express his dreams in the arts, is master of the elements,
shaping the material world to his own desired ends. The
lightning, which is force or divine energy, is now his slave
whereas once it had been the terrible weapon of Jupiter. Man
counts the stars of "heaven's utmost deep," a phrase suggestive
of the work of Herschel in his star-counts and his explorations
into the depths of stellar space. Man, too, has learned to fly,
"he strides the air." Nothing in the physical universe but
acknowledges man's mastery:

And the abyss shouts from her depth laid bare,
"Heaven, hast thou secrets? Man unveils me; I have none!"

Man ultimately, then, in Shelley's prophecy, is to be master,
through his knowledge of science, of all the forces of nature.

In the lyric antiphony which follows the Earth's long description of man's enfranchised powers, the content is scientific and the expression figurative. "The shadow of white
death has passed" from the moon, its "solid frost and sleep."
Its awakening to life and love is like the absorption of a dew-
drop by the "dissolving warmth of dawn . . . till it becomes a
wingèd mist," and at sunset

Hangs o'er the sea, a fleece of fire and amethyst.

[31] James Burnett, Lord Monboddo, *Ancient Metaphysics,* 6 vols. (London,
1795), V, 70.

This is again an instance of Shelley's employment of the phenomena of cloud formation and atmospheric electricity to symbolize the creative round of life. The cloud is the key symbol of *Prometheus Unbound* and the publication of the poem so named in the volume with *Prometheus* was the conscious or unconscious offer of a clue to the arcana of Shelley's thought. But the dual aspect of the symbol, its scientific and neo-Platonic implications both, must be perceived before the poem becomes completely intelligible.

The Moon sings to the Earth:

> Thou art folded, thou art lying
> In the light which is undying
> Of thine own joy, and Heaven's smile divine;
> All suns and constellations shower
> On thee a light, a life, a power,
> Which doth array thy sphere; thou pourest thine
> On mine, on mine!

The last four lines, as I have elsewhere remarked,[32] are clearly expressive of the forces of gravitation, electricity, and magnetism whose interplay is the "attraction" among the heavenly bodies and which the earth exerts upon the moon as the sun upon the earth. But also the first lines have I think a scientific as well as an emotional implication. "Heaven's smile divine" is the light and heat of the sun, and "thine own joy," in the light of which the earth lies, is the moon's emanations of the force and light which enfold it like an aura.

The conception of the aura, that is of soul enfolding body, which is the doctrine of neo-Platonism as of modern Theosophy, is implicit in many instances of Shelley's employment of his favorite image, the shadow. The Earth, in its song beginning

> I spin beneath my pyramid of night,

[32] *A Newton Among Poets*, p. 160.

describes accurately, as Mr. Whitehead has pointed out, an astronomical or physical phenomenon.[33] The Earth, in this passage, is likened to a youth

> Under the shadow of his beauty lying.

Here beauty, like soul or the aura, envelopes the body so that it may be thought of as the background or shadow of body. Apparently in Shelley's belief, or in his actual perception, all objects, all forms, whether plant and animal, or the seeming "mute insensate things" are in reality alive and their material substance is enveloped as with a shadow by their spiritual bodies.

The scientific implications of the Moon's reply and the characterization of her orbit as it relates to the earth I have elsewhere commented on.[34] The identification of love with physical forces—gravitation, electricity, magnetism—may be again remarked. There is also the singular thought, which Shelley elsewhere expresses, that the observer tends to become like what he contemplates, as though the soul were fed through the sense of vision, and its character determined thereby—

> As a lover or a chameleon
> Grows like what it looks upon,
> As a violet's gentle eye
> Gazes on the azure sky
> Until its hue grows like what it beholds,
> As a gray and watery mist
> Glows like solid amethyst
> Athwart the western mountain it enfolds,
> When the sunset sleeps
> Upon its snow.

The Earth's last utterance in the protracted duet of Earth and Moon ends with a curious figure:

[33] *Science and the Modern World*, p. 119.
[34] *A Newton Among Poets*, p. 163.

> O gentle Moon, thy crystal accents pierce
> The caverns of my pride's deep universe,
> Charming the tiger joy, whose tramplings fierce
> Made wounds which need thy balm.

Cavern is a familiar symbol which has been repeatedly employed throughout the poem in meanings sufficiently akin to be easily intelligible in this instance. And again to music or harmony is attributed some mystical power, on this occasion to soothe or heal. Panthea's words support the same thought:

> I rise as from a bath of sparkling water,
> A bath of azure light, among dark rocks,
> Out of the stream of sound.

Heretofore in *Prometheus Unbound* the potent power of sound has been associated with Demogorgon and ultimate realities; congruously it is in these lines prophetic of Demogorgon's reappearance to speak the peroration of the drama.

The "mighty Power, which is as darkness, . . . bursts like eclipse" from the air after "rising out of Earth" and being gathered "into the pores of sunlight." The use of "pores" in this instance, as similarly in *The Cloud,* "the pores of the ocean and shores," is scientific and is to be encountered in Beccaria[35] and Darwin. The significance of its employment is that it reveals Shelley's all but invariable perception of the phenomenal world in two aspects: its sensuous aspects appealing to eye and ear and, in the poetic depiction thereof, stirring associated emotions; and the scientific aspects which in their philosophical implications are, as in *Prometheus Unbound,* harmonized with the emotional suggestions of the sensuous imagery. In this harmony of dual implications lies the subtlety and difficulty of Shelley's verse.

Demogorgon's address to the Earth repeats an idea already encountered and explained:

[35] *Ibid.,* p. 120.

> Beautiful orb! gathering as thou dost roll
> The love which paves thy path along the skies.

The identification of love with energy, electrical energy in this instance, need not be further argued. That the Earth is a "calm empire of a happy soul" is also in accord with the neo-Platonic concept found throughout the poem, that the heavenly bodies are all individual souls. The Moon is thus addressed and

> Ye kings of sun and stars, Daemons and Gods,
>   Etherial Dominations, who possess
> Elysian, windless, fortunate abodes
>   Beyond Heaven's constellated wilderness.

This is neo-Platonic in its mythology, with an echo too, perhaps, of Newton.[36]

Again in Demogorgon's speech occurs that ambiguous allusion to the fate of the dead which we earlier encountered:

> Ye happy dead, whom beams of brightest verse
>   Are clouds to hide, not colors to portray,
> Whether your nature is that universe
>   Which once ye saw and suffered—

To which A Voice from Beneath replies:

>   Or as they
> Whom we have left, we change and pass away.

The passage is more difficult than appears on a casual reading. Does "happy dead" refer to all who have died? I think not. These are the mighty poets, peers of the Ethereal Dominations. The universe which they "once saw and suffered" I take to be the world of the divine, of reality, which they, with the insight of poets, once glimpsed. Are they dwellers in this realm of reality? Are they immortal as gods?

The question is not answered save by implication. The

---

[36] *Ibid.*, p. 167.

mighty poets are either gods or, like those whom they have
left, ordinary mortals, that is, subject to change. If they
change and pass, what do they become? The implication in
view of the neo-Platonic character of the poem throughout
and the repeated emphasis upon the round of creation is that
the souls which change and pass become again incarnate on
earth. Shelley suggests the possibility of the great poet avoid-
ing this incarnation and becoming as a god, an idea which
finds expression in *Adonais* where

> The soul of Adonais, like a star,
> Beckons from the abode where the eternal are.
>
> —ll. 494-95.

The wholly animate character of Shelley's universe is evident in Demogorgon's apostrophes to the "elemental genii"
whose homes are in "man's high mind" and in "the central
stone of sullen lead," in "Heaven's star-fretted domes" and in
the "dull weed some sea-worm battens on."[37] These are the
chemical elements which are found alike in the living matter
of the brain, in the meteorites from outer space, in every form
of matter. The universe is composed of common elements
and all these, like the "Spirits whose homes are flesh," like the
"living leaves and buds," like lightning, wind, meteors, and
mists—all are alive. So Shelley seems to say, and his poetic
practise is in accord with his profession of faith.

Demogorgon comes to declare the greatness of man, who
once was no more than

> A traveller from the cradle to the grave
> Through the dim night of this immortal day.

The night must be that which preceded the immortal day now
shining. For the rest, it is Love which has overthrown
"Heaven's despotism"; and

[37] *Ibid.,* p. 182.

> Gentleness, Virtue, Wisdom, and Endurance—
> These are the seals of that most firm assurance
> Which bars the pit over Destruction's strength.

The lines are a recapitulation of the poem's ethical philosophy: Man by self-conquest is his own liberator. And the ethics are those of Christ.

There appears in these concluding lines, however, one further philosophical idea of considerable interest.

> And if, with infirm hand, Eternity,
> Mother of many acts and hours, should free
>   The serpent that would clasp her with his length,
> These are the spells by which to reassume
> An empire o'er the disentangled doom.

The implication is of some destructive force which may ultimately be loosed to imperil the heaven of liberated man. In Act II, Scene 3, ll. 94-96 the same image was employed:

> . . . the Eternal, the Immortal,
>   Must unloose through Life's portal
> The snake-like Doom coiled underneath his throne

And again in *The Revolt of Islam:*

>   Did my spirit wake
> From sleep, as many-coloured as the snake
> That girds eternity?
>   —IV, iv, 31-33.

The origin of this serpent symbol as Shelley employs it may be various. Egyptian myth symbolizes darkness, the consumer of light, as a serpent, and in Coptic literature the Apep serpent is a monster which lies in outer darkness encircling the world and clutching its tail between its jaws. From its mouth issue "all ice, dust, cold, disease, and sickness."[38] The snake as a

---

[38] Donald A. Mackenzie, *Egyptian Myth and Legend* (London, Graham Publishing Company, 1913), pp. 159-60.

symbol of eternity is common, as in Norse mythology wherein the Midgard snake enfolds the earth in its coils. In the circle of its coils the snake fittingly symbolizes endlessness, eternity; in its poison, fatality, death, destruction.

This, however, is not the most interesting aspect of Shelley's employment of the symbol. He admits that the universe, won to order and beauty by Thought, Love, and Power, may not forever remain so. In this doubt cast upon the eternity of the Promethean plan, Shelley reflects the influence both of Indian and Platonic philosophy and of the astronomical theory of his day.

In Indian philosophy when, after incredible ages, all souls are won to Nirvana and the Maya or illusion of the material universe has vanished, the whole cycle is repeated "for the pastime of eternity." Plato, perhaps deriving the idea from Oriental philosophy, gives expression to it likewise. Shelley, too, envisages the possibility, concluding, however, that Love and Hope will again have power

> . . . to reassume
> An empire o'er the disentangled doom.

It is probable that in admitting the possibility of the destruction of the universe Shelley was thinking of the hypotheses of Newton, Herschel, and Erasmus Darwin. Newton, believing the stellar universe finite, foresaw the gravitation of matter to one dead center and the cessation of motion. Herschel in his earlier explorations of space was led to the same belief, that the stellar universe was finite, was fringed with darkness, and must sometime become, through the action of gravity in drawing all matter to a center, an inert and lifeless mass. But from this catastrophe Erasmus Darwin had predicted a rebirth:

Thus all the suns, and the planets which circle round them, may again sink into one central chaos; and may again by explosions produce a new world; which in process of time may resemble the present one, and at length again undergo the same catastrophe.[39]

It is fitting that in a poem which throughout seeks to reconcile the findings of science with the speculations of idealistic philosophy the concluding thought should be one common to both.

[39] *Temple of Nature* (London, J. Johnson, 1803), note, pp. 166-67.

CONCLUSION

I

IT HAS been early and often said that Shelley was a myth-maker, that to a degree unequalled by any other modern poet he is anthropomorphic, endowing cloud, wind, and stream each with a personality. A philosophic reason for this practise we have seen to lie in Shelley's belief in the animate character of matter. Seemingly he thought all matter literally alive and it is an easy step from such a belief to the poetic personification of all forms of matter and energy. But this faculty and prac-tise, though rare in a modern poet, do not explain wholly Shelley's creative processes in such a poem as *Prometheus Un-bound*. Therein also the creations of the mind itself are per-sonified; philosophic abstractions are projected, externalized, and become actors in a drama.

Such a process is less explicable than anthropomorphism, for the endowment of all forms of the material universe with life is a common if primitive practise, whereas the personifica-tion of abstract ideas is a much more highly sophisticated one, varying within itself, also, from the simple allegory and parable to poetic symbolism of the subtlest and most recondite order. Such as the last is Shelley's practise, one which cannot be said to be intuitive wholly, the *inspired* and unreasoned instinct of the artist, but a chosen method springing from a reasoned and articulate philosophy. Of this philosophy enough is to be found in Shelley's prose to explain his beliefs as to the nature of thought, and of the thinker as distinct from the objects of his thought.

It is evident that Shelley was a convert to the Berkeleyan psychology in which thought is held the sole reality; all we can surely know is our sensations and the operations of the mind upon these sensations—the antithesis of Locke's doctrine that the thing without is the only certainty. Thought, in this philosophy, is the reality, but there are, seemingly, different forms and degrees of thought; and there is, also, debate as to *internal* realities, such as the mind's speculations, and the *external* objects of its interest. Two passages from Shelley's *Speculations on Metaphysics* will illuminate his opinion on these issues.

Man, says Shelley, "is not a moral, and an intellectual,—but also, and preëminently, an imaginative being. His own mind is his law; his own mind is all things to him. . . . It imports little to enquire whether thought be distinct from the objects of thought. The use of the words *external* and *internal,* as applied to the establishment of this distinction, has been the symbol and source of much dispute. This is merely an affair of words, and as the dispute deserves, to say, that when speaking of the objects of thought, we indeed describe only one of the forms of thought—or that, speaking of thought, we only apprehend one operation of the universal system of [things]."[1]

The entire universe, whether *internal* or *external* in our terminology, is thought. Yet there remain, seemingly, differences among thoughts. A second citation considers this difficulty:

Thoughts, or ideas, or notions, call them what you will, differ from each other, not in kind, but in force. It has commonly been supposed that those distinct thoughts which affect a number of persons, at regular intervals, during the passage of a multitude of other thoughts, which are called *real,* or *external objects,* are totally different in kind from those which affect only a few persons, and which recur at irregular intervals, and are usually more obscure and indistinct, such as hallucinations, dreams, and the ideas of madness. No essential distinction between any one of these ideas, or any class of them, is founded on a correct observation of the nature of things, but merely on a consideration of what thoughts

[1] "Speculations on Metaphysics," *The Works of Percy Bysshe Shelley,* second part, "Essays," ed. by Mrs. Shelley (London, 1869), p. 61.

are most invariably subservient to the security and happiness of
life. . . . A specific difference between every thought of the mind,
is, indeed, a necessary consequence of that law by which it perceives diversity and number; but a generic and essential difference
is wholly arbitrary. The principle of the agreement and similarity of all thoughts, is, that they are all thoughts; the principle
of their disagreement consists in the variety and irregularity of the
occasions on which they arise in the mind. That in which they
agree, to that in which they differ, is as everything to nothing.
Important distinctions, of various degrees of force, indeed, are to be
established between them, if they were, as they may be, subjects of
ethical and economical discussion; but that is a question altogether
distinct.[2]

The statement that "important distinctions, of various degrees of force, indeed, are to be established between them" is,
I believe, most vital in considering the aesthetic problem of
the translation of philosophical ideas into poetical ideas. Similar these two kinds of ideas may be, but they ask a different
form of expression. Our distinctions of *abstract* and *concrete,*
however metaphysically questionable, are of colloquial use in
expressing this difference. The abstract thought of the philosopher is by the poet translated into concrete imagery, gain-
ing, thereby, for the commonalty of men, vastly in force.

Personification is the usual method of this translation.
Shelley's conception that man suffers from the creations of his
own thought and that salvation is to be found in his regeneration of himself is personified dramatically in the Titan,
Prometheus. Jupiter is the personification of man's inadequate
conception of God. Asia is the personification of the creative
spirit in Nature. These allegorical figures are easily intelligible
and permit that dramatic conflict which is emotionally moving. Others are not so self-evident, as instanced in Panthea,
or the Spirits of the Earth and Moon. Either the key to their
meaning is not provided or the personification is not suf-

[2] *Ibid.,* p. 59.

ficiently individual. And there is, besides, a group of ideas somewhat different in kind from those personified as the actors of the drama; for these a different, though analogous, form of expression is needed. Shelley presents his understanding of such ideas in the form of symbols.

Symbols are akin to personifications but lack the individuality, the human resemblance, with which personifications are endowed. Thus the cloud is a symbol of change and fertility; the wilderness is a symbol of the maze of the external universe or of the complexity of the individual mind; the cave is a symbol of humanity shut away from reality, or of the contemplative individual mind. The symbol is looser and more flexible than the personification and its meaning varies with its context. Symbols are, so to speak, the variables in Shelley's thought, whereas personifications are the constants. Symbols may express relationships or processes. They are the language in which are expressed thought processes themselves rather than the creations of those processes. To employ a loose but intelligible term, symbols are more *subjective* than personifications.

The need of such a symbolism for the poetical expression of Shelley's philosophy was as great as the need of symbols kindred in function in mathematics. Relationships among things, whether *objects* or *ideas,* must somehow be defined: their origins, objectives, states of being and becoming must be expressed. These may, it is true, be baldly put in the abstract terms of philosophy, but so to express them in what professes to be poetry is at once to destroy the poetical character of the medium in which they are employed. Symbols, are indeed, difficult, constituting, like the terms of mathematics, a language of their own. But once understood they are a medium, to the reader, of aesthetic satisfaction which their balder abstract phrasing denies. Even at the risk of unintelligibility the poet must employ them.

Neo-Platonic speculation had, for its convenience, built up a number of such symbols—cloud, boat, sea, cave, fountain, wilderness—and Shelley increasingly employs them, adding others which are, evidently, of his own coinage: star, dews, towers, and temples. In his earlier verse, as in the *Revolt of Islam,* he employs the symbols more often consciously in similes; but with familiarity in their use his employment is metaphorical and, also, increasingly free, the exact meaning in each instance determined by the context of the passage in which it occurs. The reader has, then, to familiarize himself with Shelley's language of the symbols or altogether fail to grasp his meaning.

Another complication lies in Shelley's employment of some of his symbols in a two-fold sense, as expressing a natural and scientific fact, relationships or changes among the processes and forces of nature; and also a philosophical fact or speculation, such as the process of spiritual creation, or the multiplicity of souls in relation to the oversoul. The symbol of the cloud, it was observed, was employed in this double signification. It may be that Shelley asks too much of the poetry lover in employing so recondite a symbolism. But that he does so and with aesthetic effectiveness once his methods are understood will, I believe, be conceded. I think it is true also that habituating himself slowly in the use of these symbols Shelley was unaware in *Prometheus Unbound* of how unintelligible they were to one who was not, like himself, versed in neo-Platonic speculations or had not followed the poet's mental development step by step. And, clearly, this is much for a poet to ask of his audience.

It is further a difficulty as also a beauty of the symbolic treatment of abstract ideas that no two readers will interpret the symbols in precisely the same way. Each will read into them the meanings which are in himself. Such a latitude of interpretation is inevitable and desirable. Great religious concepts, great philosophic ideas, great myths and poems grow in meaning with the evolution of thought. They are necessary forms, the patterns or moulds into which thought is poured. They are greater than the minds which created them, prophetic of meanings as yet unattained. So Shelley himself believed and said. Yet they must not, to serve their end, be formless, but lend themselves successively to consistent if somewhat different interpretations. Shelley's philosophy in *Prometheus Unbound* is neither formless nor inconsistent, yet to square it with the speculative needs of a later century its implications must be stressed, and the implications, it is conceded, will differ somewhat with the individual interpreters. Upon much of Shelley's meaning in his allegorical drama we may agree. Thus much, we can say, was in Shelley's mind. But what more was in his mind than this upon which we are agreed we can only individually guess. It is just to say, perhaps, that all that is in all our minds, all that is *suggested* by the poem, is within the poem. But is it necessary to believe that Shelley was wholly aware of all his implications to concede their truth and reality to us? I think not.

The Shelley lover must nevertheless concede that *Prometheus Unbound* is difficult. Subtle as its philosophy is and asking a deal of explanation, Shelley by his imagery and symbolism makes it more difficult still. The reader needs must educate himself in this symbolism until its language is familiar, after which Shelley's way of writing has a charm all its own. Shelley, himself, I believe, did not realize how difficult his form of expression was. It is true that when he wrote *Prometheus Unbound* he was indifferent to popularity; but any artist wishes an audience howsoever small and select. Shelley tells us that he wrote *Prometheus Unbound* for five or six persons. Leigh Hunt would have been one of these few, and yet Hunt, keen as was his appreciation of poetry, has left no record of his understanding *Prometheus Unbound*.   Much more than *Queen Mab, Prometheus Unbound* needed to be annotated. "It was his design," says Mrs. Shelley, "to write prose metaphysical essays on the nature of Man, which would have served to explain much of what is obscure in his poetry; a few scattered fragments of observations and remarks alone remain. He considered these philosophical views of mind and nature to be instinct with the intensest spirit of poetry."

Shelley's poetry to be understood, then, must be considered in the light of his philosophy and that philosophy he nowhere completely set down.   It is to be found in suggestions and hints and must be painstakingly composed of fragments, prose and verse conjointly being fitted together.   Aesthetically Shelley's poetry suffers from this necessity.   Poetry to have a wide appeal should be intelligible in itself.   The poet can scarcely expect that many of his readers will laboriously master a system of thought wherewith to interpret it, more especially if that system is not itself explicitly and luminously declared. For those who will do so the effort may be richly repaid, but the universality of the poet's appeal is therein limited.   In *Prometheus Unbound,* even more, the reader to understand the thought must first understand the symbolism which clothes it.

The symbolism of *Prometheus Unbound* turns, we have seen, upon the figure of the cloud, which in the world of physical nature is representative of the round of creation and decay, and which in the realm of spiritual creation symbolizes the birth of souls, their departure from the sea of universal being, and their return thereto.   The element of hydrogen liberated by the processes of plant growth passes into the upper atmosphere. Electric action fuses it with oxygen and it descends as rain to repeat its life cycle endlessly. And so likewise the human soul is drawn from its spiritual home, is incarnated for a time on earth, and ultimately returns to the place of its origin. By the employment of this symbol Shelley links and unifies his physical and his metaphysical beliefs.

Yet a figure of speech, however great its appeal to the imagination and its consequent emotional power, does not in itself solve the problems of philosophy. It may for its reader symbolize that solution if the arguments advanced have in themselves been satisfying. It remains, therefore, by way of conclusion to this study, to consider the chief heads of Shelley's philosophy in the effort to understand them and to reconcile them one with another. It need scarcely be argued at this stage that Shelley in *Prometheus Unbound* has a philosophy and one which, however recondite, is to his mind unified and consistent. Shelley's task in the poem was precisely to realize this consistency and unity in a form aesthetically satisfying.

II

The scientific scepticism of the eighteenth century emancipated men of liberal sympathies from the dark Calvinistic belief in original sin, substituting for it a belief in human perfectibility—a kindlier faith and one more in accord with the evolutionary teachings of the new science. But in so doing, basing its beliefs on the psychology of Locke and Hume, sceptical thought and humanitarian idealism rejected predestination only to accept in its place a scientific determinism which equally denied free will. There was in this denial of free will conjoined with a belief in the theory of perfectibility a philosophical inconsistency either unperceived or, when perceived, unsuccessfully solved. If the mind is not free, how can humanity become perfect unless perfectibility itself is predetermined? And in such a case why the necessity of effort? Perfection will, if predetermined, come without effort. If it is not predetermined no effort can realize it.

In *Queen Mab* Shelley believes in Necessity, the great law-giver of the universe, the scientific substitute for God. But he believes also in the Spirit of Nature and in the perfectibility of man. He endeavors to be at one and the same time scientific determinist, humanitarian, and animist. He puts together in one eloquent profession of faith all the irreconcilable beliefs of his youthful enthusiasm. His later years he spent in endeavoring to blend these beliefs into a unified and consistent philosophy, discarding some and reconciling others on a higher plane of metaphysical speculation.

It is evident that later he perceived the logical difficulties of his earlier position. He confesses in his prose his repudiation of materialism.[3] The terms material and immaterial cease to have meaning for him. The world is, as you choose, either all matter or all spirit. What you call it is of no importance provided you perceive its oneness, its complete homogeneity. In effect, Shelley came to believe that all the universe was but mind, energy, and passion—that it was, to employ the terminology which he rejected, "immaterial."

But the mind as spirit is no less bound, if its thoughts are predetermined, than is matter, if every act is predestined. Moral freedom, under whatever terminology, is the essential thing if man is to be master of his fate; and this, in his earliest thought, Shelley had denied. *Prometheus Unbound* is based implicitly on a complete recantation of this former belief. It is man's will which resists the tyranny of Jupiter. It is man's regeneration attained through suffering which frees him. Prometheus, personifying the soul of man, is his own liberator. In this concept, the will of man, if not at first

[3] See p. 100, note 5 *supra*.

wholly free is partly so, and freedom grows with use. Man evolves into freedom like grub to butterfly through his will to resist tyranny and through the triumph in himself of love over hate.

The complete reversal of Shelley's philosophical position, his substitution of an immaterial for a material concept of the world—to employ for convenience the terms which he repudiated—is evident in his reversal of the doctrine of physiological psychology of his early acceptance. In the notes of *Queen Mab* Shelley cites from Cabanis who had postulated the dependence of thought upon the physiological functions of the brain. Shelley seemingly accepts at this time the belief that mind is but a manifestation of matter, necessarily, by implication, denying all freedom of the will. But in *Prometheus* the theory is put the other way about: mind is no longer a function of matter; matter is a function of mind. This is in harmony with the Platonic belief that the only realities are intellectual, that the world of real being is in the mind. Matter is the plastic stuff which takes the shape thought creates.

Upon this belief in the power of mind depends, in *Prometheus,* the physical remaking of the world. Evil and pain existed in the reign of Jupiter because man permitted them to be; his thought was evil. When love replaces hate in the thought of Prometheus, the earth and all the forms of life are transformed. Ugly things become beautiful; energy employed to maleficent ends becomes beneficent. The Spirit of the Earth is free to play beside Asia, spirit of love and beauty in nature. It is a philosophy which does not deny the reality of evil, for reality is thought, and thought may be evil. But it denies the existence of evil as external to man, as having an independent existence in the forces of nature. All matter is energy and energy emanates from mind. Therefore as the thought is so will be the forms of the "material" universe. Evil, moreover, is relative. That which once was good becomes in time an obstacle in the achievement of a greater good and, therefore, relative to that good, evil. It is not easily supplanted even though it exists only in the mind of man, for thoughts are less easy to destroy than material things. To be destroyed it must be forgiven. Thus Prometheus supplants Jupiter only as he forgives Jupiter.

The Berkeleyan concept that all the universe is thought and the Newtonian concept that all the universe is energy are blent in Shelley's philosophy. Energy is thought or emanates from thought. Thought shapes those forms of energy which constitute the physical universe. Energy is electric and electricity is love, or, during the reign of Jupiter, hate; for energy may be misused for evil ends. In the Promethean day the forces of the physical world are beneficent because thought has become good and love is the sole principle of being.

Prometheus, freed from the tyranny of Jupiter, is reunited with Asia, spirit of creative love in nature. It is a symbol with many and varied implications, some of which may be recounted. In its simplest and most obvious sense it means no more than that man, who in some golden age lived in harmony with nature and, subsequent thereto, in discord, is now restored to his native unity. Those things which were hostile to him, all things ugly and malevolent, lay aside their unsightly masks and are seen to be beautiful and kind. There is in this, apparently, more than meets the eye: suggestion as to the nature of man and his social history. What Shelley means to stress among the various implications is, I think, by no means sure, but those that occur to me I shall briefly discuss.

Shelley's meaning would be more definite were his faith in the state of nature, of man's early innocence, more certain and its secret more definable. Perhaps the difficulty lies in my own inability to comprehend this traditional golden age. To me it seems no more than the expression of an ideal, an aspiration, which, by an accountable trick of psychology, mankind projects into the obscurity of its past rather than the uncertainty of its future. That Shelley accepts this belief is seemingly so. Men, once happy and good in the age of Saturn, became unhappy during the reign of Jupiter, and only as Prometheus is freed regain their earlier state. Their lost innocence is recaptured through knowledge, the birthright of their being.

So Shelley declares, and yet as the drama unfolds it is not apparent that this golden age is regained through knowledge but rather through the heart's conversion. Prometheus forgives his enemy, casts hate from his heart, and thereupon all evil things are turned to good and man is no longer at odds with his world. Knowledge, science, is to be the recreation of his eternity. He is to be master of the forces of nature and reconstruct the universe upon a plan "called the Promethean." Science here is man's tool in the reshaping of nature become docile and amiable. But the prerequisite harmony is born of man's change of heart. When man ceases to be at war with himself he finds that he is at peace with nature.

Shelley means, I suppose, in his characteristic Berkeleyan idiom, that there is no distinction between outer and inner. Slayer and slain, both are one, both are thought. The universe exists in man as man in the universe. Therefore only as man puts evil from himself does he put evil from the universe. I think one must have a gift for mysticism to believe this. The literal mind objects: does the earthquake cease to destroy or the lightning to strike because the soul is pure? Shelley has depicted love turned to hate as force, electricity, become the thunderbolts of Jupiter. With the destruction of Jupiter does the lightning cease? No doubt the objection is crudely put but it is with some such demurrer that the unphilosophical mind confronts the mystical assertion. How are the two points of view to be reconciled?

In these matters each must be himself the oracle as Shelley has said. A possible reconciliation lies intelligibly on a plane neither mystical nor literal. Man at war with the evil god of his creation thinks the forces of the universe hostile to him. In reality they are so while he fears them. Like the savage he seeks to propitiate them but without success. His mastery does not come until he ceases to fear them, until the god-like consciousness is his that he can do with them what he likes. With the sense of power comes power. This I believe is true, true for mankind if not wholly true for the individual. I do not know whether Shelley literally believed that lightning would cease to blast and the sea to destroy those who, having cast out fear and hate, exposed themselves to these forces. I prefer to think, inasmuch as he was scientifically minded, that he believed no such thing. But what he ardently believed was that when men ceased to fear and were assured of their intellectual mastery they would proceed to tame all natural forces and turn these to beneficent uses. Until they no longer feared, such mastery was impossible to them. It is in this sense that I interpret the union of Prometheus and Asia. The universe becomes man's to do with what he will. He is of it and master of it because his soul is at peace and his mind undistracted.

In this interpretation, the mastery of the universe through knowledge, there is implicit I think failure to comprehend any golden age of innocence. The imagination can conceive such an ideal society but only in a physical universe different from that we know. What ground have we for such a belief? Erasmus Darwin describes a phase of the earth's history free of violent storms and cataclysms in which the climate was temperate from pole to pole. Such circumstances might account for the golden age of legend, but its physical conditions must have altered to the more rigorous ones we know through the operation of natural causes. So we must believe and so Shelley must have believed despite any poetical assumptions of whatever origin whether in Plotinus, or Hesiod, or Rousseau.

It is more reasonable, I think, to suppose that his faith in the golden age of the past was due to his love of antiquity and paganism, especially the great days of Greece. The dark religion which men had made of Christianity had destroyed the nobility of the pagan world wherein, he conceived, man's relation to nature was more intimate and happy than now. He felt profoundly the unhappiness of modern men, their division from nature, and the cause of this discord he thought to be the sense of sin and the repression which Christianity inculcates of the natural and god-like in man. Mr. Massingham in a discussion of this theme says of Shelley: "Whatever the imperfections of his life, the immaturity of his ideas, the failure of his Promethean vision, he is that very artist who reconciles the Pagan with the Christian ideal; who gave all of himself away into a positive relation with life; who overcame the dualism of civilized artifice by a new unity born of his own elemental sympathy with the primitive innocence; who transcended the natural in accepting it. . . ."[4] There is much in the declared philosophy of *Prometheus Unbound* to substantiate this interpretation.

III

In his belief that all creation is alive, that earth, air, fire, and water house each its suitable form of being, Shelley goes somewhat beyond Platonism. In Platonism the heavenly bodies are divine intelligences, as are earth and moon in *Prometheus Unbound*. There are, too, in its mythology, gods,

[4] H. J. Massingham, *The Friend of Shelley, A Memoir of Edward Trelawny* (1930), p. 167. "The Romantic ideal" is further discussed, pp. 163 *et seq.*

daemons, and others, members of a hierarchy similar to that of the angels and seraphs in the Christian heaven. But matter as Plotinus conceives it is the least real of all created things, at the farthest remove from the central and life-giving One. Matter in his conception is the plastic stuff in which the creative intelligence of deity manifests itself, materializes itself, by shaping in it the forms of its thought. It is of the nature of things, in the philosophy of Plotinus, for thought so to materialize itself.

Shelley's acceptance of this belief, as far as it goes, is evident in *Prometheus Unbound*. Feeling, thought, and desire are realities which crave their material expression whether it be in art forms or in the incarnation of desires as in the lust of the furies for the blood and suffering of Prometheus. But unlike the Platonists he endows matter itself with life. It is not "unreal" as distinguished from the reality of thought. Platonist and Christian declare the baseness of flesh and matter. To the Platonist these are not real as thought is real. To the Christian they are real but base, clogs upon the spirit. In distinction from these two, Platonist and Christian, to the scientific materialist matter is the sole reality and thought itself a mechanistic by-product.

Newton's hypothesis that matter is one form of the ether, the dregs of ether so to speak, reduces the universe to a manifestation of energy. Matter is but energy in a lymphatic or frozen state and convertible back to its more active form. Ether, the mysterious fount of all energy, emanates from God and functions as light, electricity, and the spirit of animation. Everything exists, therefore, in God; but what this ether is, of which the universe consists, cannot be known save as it manifests itself in its works. Newton's hypothesis is necessarily a mystical one, but it is an advance on Platonism and neo-Platonism in that matter is reconcilable with energy, whereas in the Greek thought matter though "unreal" evidently exists of itself in some awkward and unintelligible fashion.

The importance of Newtonian theory to Shelley is evident. Not only does a conception of matter as energy reconcile Platonism with the speculations of science, but it also elucidates an obscure difficulty of Platonism itself. It achieves a monism whereas the Platonic philosophy is a dualism despite the effort to explain matter away as "unreal" or non-existent. To Newton matter is existent, is real, because it is one form or vehicle of force.

Yet Shelley's reconciliation of the doctrines of Berkeley, Plato, and Newton has, I think, only a kind of dialectical reality, if conceived wholly on the intellectual plane. It carries no emotional conviction, for the "realities" of the emotional life are inevitably bound up with "material" things. We live in a world of sensations which spring from this ambiguous matter. Our belief that matter is not "real" must, if it is more than a form of words, be an emotional conviction.

Here, apparently, we touch mysticism, which I take to be an intuitive understanding of what the reason alone cannot, with any emotional conviction, explain for us. To one who has never experienced such an intuition and cannot *feel* its truth, belief in it is impossible. Yet the evidence of philosophy and religion is clearly to the effect that this intuitive or mystical acceptance of the oneness of things is a rare but emotionally valid experience. It has been felt by many minds, these often among the best we know. Plotinus, four times, experienced it, Porphyry once. The mystical raptures of the saints, though recorded in a theological terminology, were apparently identical with it: the individual soul feels its oneness with God; all the mysteries of the universe are intelligible in a supreme emotional experience incommunicable in the exact language of the reason.

It may be said that all this is pathological, that only in some unnatural mental condition does this mystical rapture occur. If by unnatural is meant unusual, the criticism is just, but a rare or unique experience may seem to the one experiencing it more profoundly illuminating, more "real" than a thousand more usual emotions. So indeed appears the mystical experience of union with the divine: never forgotten, an eternal influence however incommunicable. It is this of which Wordsworth writes in his more inspired passages. It gives meaning to the *Lines Written Above Tintern Abbey* and to the *Ode on Intimations*. That Shelley experienced it I believe is clear from his *Hymn to Intellectual Beauty*. With Plotinus it is the One with whom the soul finds union; with the mediaeval saint it is the Blessed Bridegroom, Christ; with Wordsworth, "the spirit which rolls through all things"; and with Shelley, intellectual beauty. To each the experience is intelligible in the language with which he is most familiar, but emotionally it is much the same for all.

Nor is it an experience known only to saints, philosophers, and poets. Less articulate folk also know it. How otherwise would mystical philosophers and poets be intelligible to their readers? If the terminology of religion and mysticism offend the modern reader he may employ whatever terms he please, but as an emotional experience the sense of being at one with the universe remains none the less real. Shelley, I believe, had known it, and if so it explains his emotional acceptance of Platonism, his preoccupation with the realities beneath the appearances of things. The purely intellectual argument for the immateriality of matter, or the scientific identification of matter with energy, could have little meaning for a poet unless confirmed by such an emotional experience.

For Shelley, then, all matter is force—a belief scientifically valid; and all force is alive—a belief which has been philosophically argued. But the poetic faith in the complete animation of the universe is more than an act of reason. The imagination conceives this to be so and the emotional nature accepts this reading of life. For Shelley this belief is the source of his peculiar pantheism. In Wordsworth pantheism is the emotional belief in the oneness of things; in Shelley pantheism is more often the sense of the diverse animation of things. Philosophically these faiths are identical but the emotional emphasis differs. It is true that Shelley sometimes stresses the unity of the universe and the soul's kinship with the source of all things, but his habitual mood as a poet is his delight in the multiplicity of the forms in which the One manifests itself. Cloud, wind, tree, stream, star, sun, night, day, the hours even —personified abstractions—have for him an individual life. And in this emphasis upon multiplicity rather than unity Shelley is speaking as the artist and creator. A philosophic unity of belief was essential to his free expression as an artist, for he could not work well without a belief which satisfied his intellect. But once this intellectual creed was attained he followed his natural aptitude and poetically entered into the diverse forms of the universe. His early work is too often clouded by his philosophic doubts. Once he had allayed these he enjoyed the brief but fertile period of his poetic greatness, producing in the last four years of his life nearly all of his enduring work. Nor do I forget *Alastor* in this estimate. *Alastor* is a pale and unconvincing thing as compared, say, with *The Sensitive Plant.* And *The Revolt of Islam,* as compared with *Prometheus Unbound,* is confused and tedious.

In his mythology, Shelley, in order to endow his animate world with personable shapes, employs in effect the Rosicrucian hierarchy of gnomes, sylphs, salamanders, and nymphs.

These creatures live in the four elements as do human creatures on the face of the earth, or as do gods and daemons between earth and moon and on the heavenly spheres. That this mythology was no more than a poetic device, a convenient and traditional machinery lying to his hand cannot, I think, be affirmed. For it was evidently Shelley's belief that whatever the imagination creates has life. Imagination and thought are alive, are the shaping forces which realize themselves in the world of things. And the difference between these two worlds is seemingly no more than one of degree, of intensity of realization.

In the thought of Plotinus there are three aspects or hypostases of deity: the ineffable One who is in a sense the sum of all three and in another sense the mysterious and unqualified source of all things; second, the intellectual aspect of God which thinks and imagines; and third, the outgoing or creative force which materializes the products of thought. Seemingly this latter realization is inevitable; thought and creation are invariable adjuncts and that which exists in the mind of God must manifest itself in a created universe. Likewise in Shelley's belief the human mind works in the same fashion, if with less potency, and the imaginings of the poet are endowed with reality.

> He will watch from dawn to gloom
> The lake-reflected sun illume
> The yellow bees i' the ivy-bloom,
> Nor heed nor see what things they be;
> But from these create he can
> Forms more real than living man,
> Nurslings of immortality!
>
> —*P.U.* I, ll. 743-49.

What then is the relationship of the mind of man to the One? What does Prometheus symbolize in Shelley's philosophy? And what God, if any, replaces Jupiter upon his overthrow by Demogorgon? Satisfactory answers to these questions lead, I believe, to the heart of Shelley's philosophy as expressed in *Prometheus Unbound* and the way to them is through the conception of the triune character of God, the One. These aspects or hypostases, which have been several times defined in these pages, I wish now to consider in a somewhat different light, to debate the possibility of Prometheus, incarnation of the mind of man, being, in Shelley's belief, himself an aspect of deity. If this is so, then mankind, as summed in the beginning by Prometheus, is an aspect or hypostasis of the One, and the evolution of man is the effort to identify himself more closely with his source in the One. Man, in short, is himself God, or perhaps, more accurately, is on the way to Godhood, the goal symbolically depicted in *Prometheus Unbound* in the overthrow of Jupiter.

The four ultimate powers as they appear in the drama are these: the One, the Ineffable, identified as Love in Demogorgon's replies to Asia, the sole force unconquerable by Jupiter; Demogorgon who, at the fated time, unseats Jupiter; Prometheus, whose self conquest is the signal for Jupiter's fall; and Jupiter himself. But Jupiter is the creation of Prometheus—

I gave all he has. . . .

Jupiter, then, is less than the others and though reigning long is not ultimate and eternal. The forces which rule the world are the One, Demogorgon, and Prometheus. So put, their triune character is suggested and a consideration of their relationships strengthens the guess as to their meaning.

Of the One, save that it is identifiable with Love and that it alone is unconquerable by Jupiter, nothing is said in the poem. It is not dramatically an active force. The conflict in the drama is between Prometheus and his creation, Jupiter—

Demogorgon serving, so to speak, as arbiter of the duel and prepared to act at the behest of the victor. Jupiter looks upon him as a vassal but he proves not to be so and becomes instead the agent of Prometheus in the overthrow of Jupiter. He, then, like Prometheus is unconquerable save by Love, and the two are in this respect identifiable with the One. The similarity of the conception to the hypostases of the Platonic trilogy is evident, and an examination of the functions of Prometheus and Demogorgon strengthens the likeness and brings out the philosophic implications of Shelley's conception.

If Prometheus be thought of as the intellectual hypostasis, Demogorgon corresponds to the third or outgoing hypostasis of deity, that which realizes in the world of outward things the ideas of the second, or intellectual, hypostasis. Demogorgon we have thought of as Necessity and so in this interpretation he remains; not Necessity in the lower and mechanistic sense, but the Necessity which, by the law of the One's being, manifests itself in the realization or materialization of thought. Ideas must find their material expression and to this end Demogorgon is the agent. So conceived he must unseat Jupiter despite the spirit of forgiveness in which Prometheus would spare his foe. For Jupiter is the creation of the Titan, the child of Prometheus' thought, the outgrown deity of man's worship. Prometheus, in forgiving Jupiter, of necessity destroys him; as when a man forgiving himself the faults of his past and no longer the victim of remorse, thereby frees himself from that past and learns to forget. Jupiter is the creation of thought, more real than something made of matter or flesh. Only forgiveness can and must destroy him. Upon the expression of that forgiveness the action of Demogorgon is inevitable.

If this reading is correct, Prometheus, personifying the race of man, the spirit or oversoul of man, is god-like even in his imperfections; and, as he becomes more perfect in the spirit of Christ, is drawn closer to God, attaining that reunion with the One which is the soul's desire. Why then the imperfection of Prometheus, why sin and error? Therein is the mystery which lies at the heart both of Christianity and Platonism. In Christianity God is symbolized as incarnate in Christ, in expiation of man's sins and as a means to his salvation. If Prometheus, the mind of man, be thought of as the second or intellective attribute of deity, incarnating itself whether of necessity or choice, the resemblance of this philosophy to the Christian doctrine of the incarnation of Godhead in Christ is manifest. Man, who is God, is also, in this conception, Christ who endures the crucifixion and redeems the world through love. The Christian doctrine of the trinity derives from and is more intelligible in the terms of Platonic philosophy. The mystical doctrine of the atonement would seem likewise more intelligible in symbolism such as Shelley employs. But that Shelley consciously interprets Christian beliefs, save as he adopts the ethics of Christ as a means to the freeing of Prometheus, does not appear.

If the doctrine of the atonement in Christian theology is a difficult one, so similarly in Platonism is the incarnation of the souls, who from some inner and mysterious necessity leave their heavenly abode and undergo the crucifixion of this life until, having relearned virtue, they again become a part of the One. Plotinus gives several reasons for the "fall" of the souls and in the multiplicity of his explanations confesses his inability to reconcile a world of sin and pain with an all-perfect God. In effect, if not in his terms, Plotinus postulates an imperfect, an evolving God.

Evolutionary doctrine as implicit in the scheme of Platonism derives, it may be, from Oriental sources, for in the Hindoo mythology the round of creation and decay, of cycles

of evolution and attained perfection, is endless. The souls
thus learn wisdom through error; understand virtue from
having practised vice; or, seeking self-expression in the pride
of free will, learn that only as the soul chooses good is it really
free. Whatever the cause for the incarnation of souls and
their return to God, it springs from some inner and mysterious
necessity beyond which speculation cannot go. Yet it is notable
that such a theology is reconcilable on a temporal plane with
the evolutionary theory of science. In each of its cycles life
evolves from imperfection to perfection. But theology ascribes
an end to each cycle, whereas science in general is concerned
with the process of the cycle itself, and the ever nearer approach to a goal never completely attained. If it conceives the
goal as attained it supposes a universe at last inert and dead
which may or may not, through forces within itself, start the
process anew.

It is on some such ground that Shelley's theology, if derived, as seems to be the case, from neo-Platonism, is reconcilable with the theory of evolution as taught by Erasmus
Darwin. Darwin, as a scientist, contemplates the running
down of the cosmic clock, the approach to one dead center of
the innumerable stars and then through "fierce explosions" the
creation of a new universe and the repetition of the process; a
contingency at which Shelley glances in the conclusion to
Prometheus Unbound, wherein he says that the virtues of
hope, love, wisdom, and endurance will build a new universe
from the "disentangled doom." In the cycles of such a theology, evolution, though not endlessly progressive, is the process
of each individual cycle. Therein is reconcilable also Shelley's
apparent belief in a golden age of the past, for in the infinite
history of creation perfection has been attained many times
and will be again attained. A passage from Medwin's *Conversations of Lord Byron* is illuminating, for if it does not, as

I suspect, originate in some speculation of Shelley's, it at any rate expresses a theory with which Shelley must have been familiar. Byron is recorded as saying:

> We are at present in the infancy of science. Do you imagine that, in former stages of this planet, wiser creatures than ourselves did not exist? All our boasted inventions are but shadows of what has been—the dim images of the past—the dream of other states of existence. Might not the fable of Prometheus, and his stealing the fire, and of Briareus and his earth-born brothers be but traditions of steam and its machinery? Who knows whether, when a comet shall approach this globe to destroy it, as it often has been and will be destroyed, men will not tear rocks from their foundations by means of steam, and hurl mountains, as the giants are said to have done, against the flaming mass?—and then we shall have traditions of Titan again, and of wars with Heaven.[5]

The freeing of Prometheus would symbolize, then, in one aspect, the triumph of science, man's mastery of force and matter.

The conception of a golden age in the infancy of the world is one harmonious both with Platonic and French Revolutionary philosophy. It was congruous, too, with scientific speculation in Shelley's time which believed that there had been a deluge or a similar catastrophe which destroyed ancient civilizations of a high order. The process might indeed have been many times repeated, a cyclical evolutionary theory kindred to the cyclical theory of Platonic and Indian philosophy. Metaphysically the concept harmonizes with the notion of the One, or deity, realizing itself in an evolving material universe. But the process is wearisome and futile if thought of as repeated. The realization of the concepts of the One should, therefore, be an endless process, and so, I take it, Shelley depicts it in *Prometheus Unbound*. Emotionally and aesthetically he thus conceives the Promethean plan. If, metaphysically, he

[5] (London, 1824), p. 185.

conceives the process as finite and endlessly repeated, the concession is made for philosophic consistency. Emotionally he
believes in man's endless advance in science and the arts once
he is morally free. Yet it must be admitted that the golden
age or ages of the past are, for Shelley's philosophy, a vestige
of tradition better ignored and which but for the seeming support lent by science, he must have discarded as inconsistent
with an evolutionary conception of life which could ethically
satisfy.

Shelley's interest in evolutionary theory is more evident in
his description of the stellar universe than of life forms. The
growth of solar systems from the primordial nebulous stuff is
depicted with an exactness which evidences his knowledge of
Laplace and Sir William Herschel. In his account of organic
evolution he remarks on prehistoric monsters and on the an-
cestors of man who were "mortal but not human," a phrase
suggesting that he subscribed to the theory of Helvetius that
man was descended from a tribe of monkeys which had
learned the use of their thumbs; or that he believed in prehistoric races destroyed by some cataclysm of nature.

The growth of stars and the descent of man are, however,
in Shelley's philosophy but superficial evidences of an evolutionary theory whose originality lies in this, that it is mental
and moral. The outer changes of the universe and of man
are but manifestations of inner growth. This is in accord with
Shelley's Platonic philosophy and in part with the evolutionary
theory of Erasmus Darwin. Darwin's vitalistic theory ascribes
the evolutionary changes in life forms to some force within
the animal and plant. It postulates, in effect, free will rather
than determinism, and in this respect is the antithesis of the
evolutionary theory of Charles Darwin, which is mechanistic.

Erasmus Darwin's theory of evolution is kin to the vitalistic
doctrine of Bergson. Life is thought of as a conscious and

adaptable force which experiments with matter and learns in the process how best it may reach its ends. Shelley in his stress upon the shaping power of mind is thus in accord with both Darwin and Platonism. Yet he carries the theory one step further than does Darwin, though still in harmony with the implications of Platonism. The significant evolution of man is to Shelley ethical. As man grows in goodness, in love, he frees himself from his past and is increasingly master of his material universe. Shelley's idea I think is most intelligibly expressed in terms borrowed from Platonism. Man as God in the making becomes God when he attains perfect love. He is then identified with the first hypostasis of the One—love, truth, beauty. In this identification with the One through love, the intellective hypostasis which is the second aspect of divinity becomes wholly free also and whatever it creates in thought is materially realized in earthly forms. But the moral growth is basic in man's evolution towards God. From moral freedom all else follows.

Shelley's conception of the universe is superficially Manicheistic. Good and evil are in eternal conflict. These forces exist in the divine mind itself and are expressed in its works. But when to this conception is added an evolutionary belief, good becomes rather the goal, the triumphant issue from evil; and evil is such only as it is the past whence good, with difficulty, issues. There is, then, relativity in ethics. A primitive conception of God (good in its time) becomes evil as it hampers the growth of a better God. Hence the past is, in the main evil, because of the obstacles which it (inevitably) sets up in the attainment of a better future. That reality is thought, that the forms of the material world are but the visible manifestations of thought, makes the conflict of good with evil none the less real, for thought is less destructible than the forms of matter, and an "inner" conversion is more difficult to effect than the destruction of the body.

The evolutionary character of Shelley's philosophy is somewhat obscured by the dramatic necessities of *Prometheus Unbound*. The slow processes of man's evolution from brute to God cannot be detailed. It is the dramatic, the catastrophic, moment when man ceases to be man and becomes God that is seized and symbolized in the destruction of Jupiter. In so depicting the evolution of man the conflict of good and evil within men is objectified, is made emotionally compelling. Experience is foreshortened and the events of aeons are crowded into the moment. There is inevitably an inherent falsification of fact in such a dramatization. But the needful implications to rectify this emphasis are resident in the drama itself.

Shelley's God is, in reality, an imperfect God, a God who strives to become and who wrestles both with his own nature and with the recalcitrant forms of a "material" universe. Think of the universe as "immaterial" and the struggle remains the same. God then struggles in the evolution of his own thought with the less perfect thoughts of his past. These must be relinquished to be replaced. If they are evil, and as less perfect they are relatively evil, they must be forgiven to be destroyed. Thought is reality. Heaven and hell, beauty and ugliness, exist within the mind. Evil, so conceived, endures until it grows into good, for thought evolves precisely as does the "material" universe which "realizes" it. All this is, no doubt, somewhat tenuous but nevertheless intelligible and explicitly latent in Shelley's symbolism.

What then of time in this history? Upon the destruction of Jupiter, time is borne "to his tomb in eternity," and the new golden age is characterized as timeless. Perfection is attained, terrestrial evolution has ceased, and the dream of the creative force is thus far realized. Yet the spirits of the human mind are depicted as setting forth into the chaos which skirts the organized cosmos and as there building other worlds after a plan "called the Promethean." New arts and aesthetic satis- factions are also promised, and life, save for its joy and free- dom from ancient ills, moves evidently after an intelligible earthly fashion. Metaphysically it is difficult to reconcile this conception with any timeless universe. Moreover the threat of destruction and a repetition of the life cycle is definitely envisaged in the drama's concluding lines.

Shelley faces, in short, the usual paradox of metaphysical speculation. Insofar as the scheme of all creation, past and present, may be thought of as existing in the mind of God— the intellectual hypostasis of Platonic terminology—his being may be thought of as timeless. But in the materialization of ideas through the creative agent (Demogorgon in the drama) there is necessarily sequence and therefore time. The mate- rialization is not, that is, complete and synchronous with the inception of the idea in the mind of deity; if indeed it is possible to think of the entire scheme of creation as springing like a full-blown rose from the imagination of God. Time, if no more than a sequence of thought, is necessary to human understanding, and to speak of timelessness is to employ a form of words humanly unintelligible. The human mind is caught in a dilemma from which there is no genuine, but merely a dialectical, escape. To say that God is timeless is intelligibly to say no more than that the creative mind is completely prophetic and knows in each step of the unfold- ing drama its inevitable consequence. Incidentally, such a concept denies wholly any freedom of the will, any chance of variation. The universe becomes a closed circle, a manifesta- tion wholly predetermined. This conception is at odds with Shelley's portrayal of Prometheus both in the Titan's conquest of Jupiter and in the pursuits of the Promethean day. The concession to eternity is, I think, more dialectical than real.

Possibly, for philosophical consistency, a distinction may be drawn in the third act between the liberated Prometheus who, reunited with the One, is timeless, and the universe in which he unfolds himself in time. Man in the Promethean day is depicted as

> Sceptreless, free, uncircumscribed . . .

but he is yet man

> Nor yet exempt, though ruling them like slaves,
> From chance, and death, and mutability.

Man's life in short remains, though happier and freed from pain and evil, otherwise as it is now. In the exercise of his creative powers in the arts and sciences man pursues his way in an evolving universe, one, too, which may sometime be destroyed. But from this destruction the enduring power of Prometheus will create a new material universe through the powers of

> Gentleness, Virtue, Wisdom, and Endurance.

IV

Byron, who said of Shelley that he was fuller of poetry than any man now living,[6] deplored his metaphysical and Utopian themes. Yet concern for humanity was Shelley's profoundest affection from first to last. Utopias were his refuge from the too bitter reality of the human lot. And metaphysics to such a mind as his was inescapable, for no hope in the future of man could be held unless reasonable and intelligible in the scheme of things. That there may be hope of man's future, his origin and past must be explained, the good and evil in him justified. The philosophical mind demands an

[6] *Ibid.*, p. 236.

explanation of the whole before it can explain and justify the parts. Byron got along very well without a unified philosophy; but not so Shelley, whose intellectual history is the story of his efforts to fuse and unify his various beliefs.

Prometheus Unbound therefore is Utopian as *Queen Mab* is Utopian but with a far more solid basis in philosophic thinking. The logical inconsistencies of the earlier poem are ironed out, and science and idealism are reconciled in an immaterial philosophy which is unified, intelligible, and consistent with itself. The way in which an early belief is modified or reconciled to a later philosophic necessity in this evolution of Shelley's thought is exceedingly interesting, notably in his adaptation of his humanitarian beliefs to this philosophic background.

The "religion of humanity" of Paine's coinage was the religion of the free-thinking reformers of French Revolutionary days to whom Shelley was intellectual heir. As Shelley first conceived the human drama, mankind, potentially good, was opposed to God, the evil force in the world whose ministers were priests and kings. Man's greatness lay in his defiance and the intangible hope that somehow, sometime, he would destroy kings and priests and become free. The God of this contest is the God of the Church and it is hard to say whether Shelley believed in his reality or how, if believing, this God was reconcilable with belief in a Spirit of Nature and with the goodness innate in man.

Clearly God's place in the scheme of things and his very nature must be defined before the way to philosophical consistency became manifest. "God" in the ecclesiastical sense was at war with the Spirit of Love in Nature. God was, thus, in reality the evil spirit of a Manicheistic dualism. All this is a matter of definition. Shelley quarreled with the term "God" because of the associations of cruelty and intolerance with which his worship was allied. Especially Shelley hated institutional and traditional Christianity, believing it, like Voltaire, Godwin, and others, to be the most intolerant and cruel of faiths.

In *Queen Mab* Shelley depicts Christ as a hypocrite, as one professing meekness and love while inciting his followers to intolerance and cruelty. But with more mature study of Christ's life and teachings Shelley became a convert to the ethics of Christ and made henceforth a distinction between Christ's teachings and institutional Christianity. The lines in *Prometheus Unbound* are explicit in this distinction. Christ's name has become a curse by reason of the acts committed by his professed followers. The most intolerable of the visions of Prometheus is that of the crucified youth who looks upon the cruelty of man committed in his name. Browning and Francis Thompson who declared Shelley a convert to Christianity were correct if by this is meant conversion to Christ's ethics; but wholly wrong in predicting that Shelley could ever have been a professing Christian. To the last Shelley maintained the distinction between the teachings of the founder of Christianity and the acts of the warring churches committed at the instigation, as he conceived it, of the devil god of their own creation. The Jupiter of *Prometheus Unbound* is the God of Christianity, of Mohammedanism, the God of many names, the imperfect creation of man. Christ is the incarnation of the spirit of love, of the One, the ultimate ruler of the universe.

Prometheus himself is a symbol of Christ, the spirit of love crucified for man's salvation. But Prometheus is more than Christ. True, he becomes master of the world only as the spirit of Christ realized in him enables him to overthrow the God of his earlier Creation. Good expels evil. Yet there are other than ethical elements in his nature. In him is the pagan love of and identification with nature—Asia. And in him, too, is the thirst for knowledge, man's scientific and enquiring spirit. More than all he is the creative spirit of man, which builds a new world based on Christian humanitarian ethics, the Greek love of nature and beauty, and the speculative and experimental scientific research of the modern man. Only as these elements find their perfection and balance, is the spirit of man emancipated and the golden age attained.

The emancipation of man is through his own effort, the regeneration of his nature from within. He is a free, or partially free, agent. Shelley's position on this point is one of the greatest philosophical interest and is reconcilable both with his evolutionary tenets and his Platonism. But it was a position not easily arrived at, for Shelley began intellectually as a disciple of Locke and Hume and of the Revolutionary philosophers whose psychology was based on theirs. Absolute determinism is the philosophy of Holbach whom Shelley quotes with such enthusiasm in the notes to *Queen Mab*. Therein every mote in the dust storm describes a predetermined course. Likewise every act of every member of a mob is conditioned by his previous acts and all the complicated forces of his environment.

Shelley as a youth found this belief not irreconcilable with his faith in perfectibility, but his maturer thought repudiated it. Perhaps the evolutionary theories of Erasmus Darwin were instrumental in this change; perhaps, also, Shelley's growing faith in Platonism with its emphasis upon intuitive knowledge. In Darwin the adaptation of plant and animal to its environment springs from its voluntary choice. The animal attains a better life for itself from an inner urgency, by acts instinctive or intuitive in their origin, implanted by the spirit of nature. Likewise in Platonism, though material determinism plays its subordinate part in the scheme of things, man,

the highest of earthly creatures, is free, or partly free, growing
in freedom as he prefers good to evil. In *Julian and Mad-
dalo* (1818-19), a poem of the same period as *Prometheus Unbound,* occurs a passage so pertinent to this discussion of the
will in relation to evil that I cite it here:

> It is our will
> That thus enchains us to permitted ill.
> We might be otherwise; we might be all
> We dream of happy, high, majestical.
> Where is the love, beauty and truth we seek,
> But in our mind? and if we were not weak,
> Should we be less in deed than in desire?
>
> . . . .
>
> . . . . We are assured
> Much may be conquered, much may be endured
> Of what degrades and crushes us. We know
> That we have power over ourselves to do
> And suffer—what, we know not till we try;
> But something nobler than to live and die.
> So taught those kings of old philosophy,
> Who reigned before religion made men blind;
> And those who suffer with their suffering kind
> Yet feel this faith religion.
> —*Julian and Maddalo,* ll. 170-191.

Shelley's avowal of his indebtedness to the "old philosophers"
suggests the Platonists as the source of his doctrine of the freedom—or partial freedom—of the will.

> All beings are enslaved that serve things evil.

So Demogorgon answers Asia when she asks whether Jupiter
is free and omnipotent. Prometheus, therefore, as he is first
depicted in the drama is neither wholly enslaved nor wholly
free. The will to resist, to attain ultimately his desires for
man, is the sign of his divinity and freedom. But he is enslaved by his past, by his own thoughts. Jupiter is the product

of that thought, a deity created when Prometheus, the mind of man, was but partly evolved. He must outgrow that ideal before he is wholly free. When he can repudiate his memories, the earlier creations of his thought, the past drops from him and he is enfranchised.

That the physical universe should at once respond to the thought of a liberated Prometheus, should in an instant be transformed, its evil changed to good and its ugliness to beauty is, if too literally regarded, a mystical conception. But here again, as in the catastrophic delineation of the evolution of Prometheus himself, the dramatic form is somewhat misleading. Time clearly is necessary to the unfolding of the Promethean universe, howsoever Shelley may symbolically depict time as borne to his tomb in eternity. It is in time, then, that the thought of Prometheus reshapes the world, and it is by the employment of science that natural forces are made to respond to his will. The emphasis which Shelley places upon science together with the arts as the recreations of liberated man would have no meaning were the conceptions of Prometheus instantaneously realized and did eternity exist in the ever present now. The destruction of evil and ugliness is, for dramatic effect, compressed, but the process must in actuality be an evolution of Prometheus himself. As he grows in goodness so does the external universe grow in beauty. In presenting his philosophic theme dramatically Shelley's symbolism, to be understood and to be made consistent, must be so interpreted.

Shelley's emphasis in *Prometheus Unbound* is upon the moral evolution of man. The religions of humanity mark the stages of man's emergence from the brute. As they are outgrown they are with difficulty cast aside and replaced with new and better ideals. So, evidently, in Shelley's eyes institutional Christianity is inadequate to modern man, whereas the ethics of Christ, which are those of love, remain as the ideal of man's moral perfection. And upon man's moral improvement depends his physical improvement and that of all the natural creation. In this philosophy mind, not matter, is the central reality. Matter is shaped by thought, is subservient to it; is, when mind is free, wholly plastic. The belief is in keeping with Platonism and reconcilable with a partial material determinism, a determinism which becomes weaker as man becomes spiritually more and more free.

Shelley's philosophy as thus defined has its affiliations with various cults and philosophies old and new. It is a reconciliation of the various ideas in which Shelley had to believe: his faith in man's perfectibility; his belief in intuition; in the Platonic world of ideas, intuitions of which are the guide to truth; belief in the intellect as the tool of the higher intuition, an important though secondary mental attribute; the recognition of matter as real, because but a form of force, and plastic in the hands of man as he realizes his divine powers. The end is man's perfect mastery of his world, and the identification of Prometheus, the mind of man, with divinity itself, which out of some mysterious necessity, or for the pastime of eternity, shapes the objects of its thought in the material universe. Art in this synthesis is at one with religion.

But why, the modern doubter asks, all this painful round of human effort to reattain union with the One? The One is all-loving and all-good and yet permits a world of imperfections, an evolutionary world, to be sure, and with promise of perfection. The answer of neo-Platonism to this riddle we have seen: it declared variously that evil is necessary that good may be known by contrast; that the souls self-willed seek experience, learn the folly of their acts, and return at last to the One; or that in some mystical sense this experience is inevitable and that though they think themselves free in their choice of the lesser good, the souls are not free in reality. In these too numerous explanations the effort to reconcile a perfect God with an imperfect world is not wholly successful.

There are, I believe, two ways out of this dilemma, one the modern belief in the evolution of God himself. He is conceived of as a force endeavoring to realize itself, as life striving to subdue matter to its will. God in this belief is not omnipotent but strives to become so. There are philosophic difficulties here in accounting for the dualism of things and the origin of the conflict. To think of God or the forces of life as coming into being through some fortuitous concourse of atoms is unsatisfying to the mind, whose desire is for purpose, law, unity. Neo-Platonism, as we have seen, though basing its philosophy upon an evolutionary hypothesis, makes this evolution subordinate to, a phase of, the higher timeless unity of perfection. It says, virtually, that the imperfections of an evolving world are due to the will of God and are, in some mystical sense which man cannot wholly understand but in which he must believe, wholly right.

Neither the mysticism of neo-Platonism, which demands an act of faith, a surrender to the divine will, nor the modern belief in an evolving and imperfect God, is philosophically satisfying. No answer to the riddle of the universe has been nor perhaps ever can be so. Yet the implications of Shelley's philosophy as set forth in *Prometheus Unbound* evidence his attempt to reconcile the neo-Platonic doctrine with the evolutionary theory, and wrest from this reconciliation if not wholly a philosophical yet an ethical satisfaction. It is in his conception of Prometheus, the mind of man, in its relation to the One that is to be found his justification of evil in a universe created by a perfect God, an evil which is convertible to good.

To the individual, evil and pain are wholly intolerable only as they affect others. For himself he can usually endure them and justify them on one of two grounds: either that he has brought them upon himself, or that through them he has learned wisdom. Philosophically, perhaps, he should in like manner extenuate the pain of others, conceiving them to be as himself. What is true of him as a member of a corporate body should be true of all. But in reality he rails at God for this cruelty in life and cannot forgive for others what he can pardon in his own lot. For these others he necessarily conceives God as a being outside of man and imposing suffering from the seat of authority. For himself the relation with God is more intimate. If a religious nature he may find the spirit of God within himself and feel that as he suffers so God suffers; he identifies himself with God.

Shelley in his conception of Prometheus identifies the Titan with mankind as a whole and also with the intellectual hypostasis of deity. Mankind is God himself, God who suffers a self-imposed evolution, for some mysterious reason—to acquire experience, to realize himself. The reason remains obscure. No more can be said than that it is of the nature of things that God-Man should so impose multiplicity upon himself. This is the inevitable and ultimate axiom or hypothesis behind which speculation cannot go. But if not wholly satisfying in a philosophic sense it is ethically far more so than is the conception of a God residing without man's universe and imposing upon him such a life as men know, with its evil and its pain. Experience freely sought, even though painful, is explicable. This is Shelley's conception, if Prometheus be thought of as God himself, the One who imposes multiplicity upon his unity, and from this multiplicity evolves again into unity. The other conception of deity, that of traditional Christianity, is of a God existing in himself and imposing his painful and inexplicable decrees upon suffering man. Such a theology Shelley sets forth in the conflict of Jupiter and Prometheus. This God who is without, Prometheus destroys, and discovers that he himself is God. God is not outside man's universe but exists in man himself. Individual men are the constituent parts of God.

In his conception Shelley, if he does not depart from neo-Platonism, at least subordinates its cyclical theory, its stress upon the ultimate union with the One and the subsequent repetition of the creative process. In the cyclical theory is resident an inherent futility. Men can conceive of an evolutionary process infinite in extent, with ever new goals upon the horizon as each one is attained, an endless process of creative and aesthetic satisfactions. But to think of the process as finite, as ending in static perfection, is repugnant to the sense of life itself. The game has again to be played over with the same conclusion as before. The imagination faints at the thought of these endless and futile gyrations. Whatever satisfaction the religious mind may derive from their contemplation, the aesthetic mind will have none of them. To it the creative unfolding of the intellect must be infinite if it is to satisfy.

The philosopher may joyfully contemplate an eternity of reflection. Not so the creative artist. The essence of his pleasure is the continuous unfolding of his perceptions of beauty, of the invention of new forms through which his aesthetic sense may grow, its internal evolution being reflected in the outward forms which it creates. The Platonist believes that these forms are but approximations of the ideals already existent in the mind of the One; that the artist in his work increasingly identifies himself with the One and that his goal, like the philosopher's, is his ultimate merging with the One. I do not think that the artist understands, or understanding, approves such a consummation. Cessation of activity is to him death;

the pursuit of beauty, endless. His ideal of the One, could he define it, or did he care to define it, would be a God of an ever evolving, ever growing beauty. A wholly perfect beauty, one completely achieved, would not satisfy. There must beyond every achievement be the possibility of one better. Artist and philosopher cannot, therefore, look eye to eye on this union with the One. Whatever the artist's nominal acceptance of the One—this necessitated, if he is of philosophic mind, by the desire only for roundness and consistency of doctrine—his real concern is with the process of arriving, not the goal itself. So it is apparent in Shelley, in his picture of the Promethean world. Theoretically man has identified himself with the One, with God. But though ethically perfected, men are still creatures of passion and their pleasure lies in the discoveries of the arts.

I think it can be argued pertinently that this endless exploration of the arts is itself necessary to the contemplative mind which, otherwise, would sometime come to an end of its contemplations however protracted. If the aim of experience is to provide food for thought, experience must be infinite, must endlessly evolve, else thought itself have an end and the universe of the objects of reflection and the philosopher, reflecting upon them, become fixed in death. The desire for the absolute, for the One, is in part the stimulus to an unattainable goal, one which recedes to the degree with which it is approached; and in part only a natural and human desire for rest. To the weary mind, endless life, endless effort and pain, are horrible to contemplate. To the mind rested and rejoicing in the desire to create, life must be infinite to realize its desire.

This creative and aesthetic spirit, one of endless progression, is that on which Shelley dwells in the fourth act of Prometheus. If catastrophe is envisaged and the repetition of the cycle, it is but a philosophic concession. Shelley is not interested in the attainment of perfection but in the infinite progress towards such perfection, a goal forever removed and unattained. Or perhaps it would be more exact to say that the attainment of ethical perfection—symbolized in the freeing of Prometheus—is the precursor of the infinite realization in creative and aesthetic satisfactions of the liberated spirit of man.

Is this idea wholly reconcilable with the idea of deity, as personified in Prometheus, the spirit of man, imposing experience upon itself? It is so, I think, if the realization of God's intellection is a created and an infinite process. God's thought cannot, in that case, ever be complete and static, for its materialization would then be a finite process. Thought must itself grow forever, must forever evolve, for if not, there is sometime an end and either a repellent torpor of perfection, or a futile repetition of the round. Shelley's concessions to neo-Platonic theory are in this respect, it seems to me, verbal only. The "disentangled doom" he accepts as a theoretic possibility, but his emotional interest lies in an eternal process of ever creative activity and aesthetic expression, of Man-God "realizing" himself endlessly.

Whether our world will be interested in such a philosophy, whether its solutions and its terms will appeal to the modern mind, cannot be predicted. Shelley's philosophy is subtle and the symbolic expression of it difficult. It employs ideas which are foreign to modern thought. Yet, together with these ideas so anciently derived are others now very much alive. The immateriality of matter, the stress upon evolution, the humanitarian note—these ideas are more widely dispersed in our day than in Shelley's. He anticipates our thought, our emphasis. Most of all, in his concern with the creative and aesthetic powers of men, the satisfaction which he derives in contemplating a heaven active in the pursuit of the arts and the control of natural forces, he should strike a sympathetic chord in the heart of today. A holiness aloof from life, a merely contemplative goodness, seems to the modern mind mediaeval, reminiscent of anchorites and of a sanctity which has no place for the strenuous life. The way to its God is through the work of human betterment, through the mastery of natural forces by science, and through the endless unfolding of man's power to conceive and realize beauty. To the "good" of Platonism Shelley adds "truth and beauty" as ideals equally desirable, ideals attainable only by the active life, and with joy found in the doing. In these respects, in this "activism," Shelley is our contemporary; perhaps a prophet of futurity.

INDEX